The Business Sergeant's
FIELD MANUAL

Military Grade Business Execution
Without the Yelling and Push-ups

By Chris Hallberg

TODAY'S DATE: _____

FIELD MANUAL OWNER'S NAME: _____

☐ **I BOUGHT THIS FIELD MANUAL FOR MYSELF**
(I'm ready to take complete control of my team's future!)

☐ **MY BUSINESS BATTLE BUDDY** _____
bought it for me because I'm important to them and they really want to see
me achieve my goals and dreams.

ACKNOWLEDGMENTS

To my many mentors, clients, peers, and friends: This book would not be possible without you and your roles shaping my military, paramilitary, and professional life experiences. You know who you are. **Thank You!**

To my family: my wife of 20 years, Melissa, sons Hunter and Hayden, father Lars (U.S. Army Vet) and stepmother Terrie, mother Cheryl and stepfather Robert (U.S. Air Force vet), brothers Erik and Jon, stepsisters Jennifer and Jessica and all the rest of our awesome extend family, you have always believed in me, and I thank you deeply for that.

To my good friend and mentor Gino Wickman, thank you for your brilliant gift of EOS® and to the world class community of EOS Implementers™ who continue to amaze me with their abundance mindset, collaboration, and support on this amazing and wondrous journey to mastery that will never be achieved. Wax on, wax off.

EOS®, The Entrepreneurial Operating System® and Traction® are registered trademarks
of Gino Wickman. All rights reserved. Accountability Chart™, Clarity Break™,
Compartmentalize™, Core Focus™, Core Target™, LMA™, The Level 10 Meeting™, The
Vision Component™, The Vision/Traction Organizer™, V/TO™, EOS Process™ , The
People Analyzer™, The 90-Day World™, The 90 Minute Meeting™ are trademarks of
Gino Wickman used with permission.

Business Sergeant Books
www.bizsgt.com

Printed in the United States of America
ISBN 978-0-9991018-0-3 (Paperback)

Editing by Jake Brown, Al Desetta, and Dave Flomberg

Cover Design: concept by Chris Hallberg, design by Keith Roberts & Thomas Hutton
Text design, graphics, and composition by Thomas Hutton
Printed and Distributed by Bookmasters

TABLE OF CONTENTS

FOREWORD

I'm so glad and proud that Chris has invested the time to share his experience and this powerful message with you.

This book is a rare treat. At EOS Worldwide, we have almost 200 extraordinary EOS Implementers around the world who work hands-on with their clients, helping them implement EOS in their businesses. By fully implementing EOS® (The Entrepreneurial Operating System®) in their businesses, our clients realize amazing results: growth, better life balance, increased profits, and the ability to make a huge impact on their employees, their customers, and the world.

Every one of our EOS Implementers has their own style that makes them unique. Chris Hallberg is truly one of our best EOS Implementers. The reason this book is a rare treat is that Chris shares his real-world life experience and stories of how his clients have benefited from EOS and his uncommon background.

Chris's military, law enforcement, and business background, along with his intense, disciplined, fun and energetic style, makes for a thrilling experience for his clients and for you as the reader.

Chris shares his extensive, emotional, and inspiring background with stories, insights, and teaching that have made him who he is.

This book will help you become a more disciplined leader and build a great organization.

Enjoy!

Gino Wickman

Author of *Traction* and Creator of EOS Worldwide

INTRODUCTION
ENLISTING TO BECOME A BUSINESS SERGEANT

A-ten-tion!

My name is Chris Hallberg, and I'm known in entrepreneurial circles as the "Business Sergeant." As a leadership and management coach to entrepreneurs and their leadership teams, my job is to help you get control of your business, so you can achieve your mission—it's that simple. How do I do that? By distilling the best practices of military and para-military organizations and helping you apply them to your business. I believe that a military team-building mindset plus a proven business operating system = a better, faster, and more predictable way to achieve business success.

The military has a system for everything, and those systems can help you harness the energy of your employees and lead them to greatness. This book is simply a modified version of that military training, designed to help entrepreneurs of small and medium sized businesses, their leaders and managers, and even much larger organizations in the corporate world. These concepts apply in any field to gain optimal performance from their business. Because without a proven system, I find it's very difficult to consistently run a business of any size successfully.

To be clear, *The Business Sergeant's Field Manual* is not about my career in elite military units and all the unbelievable things I did in the most dangerous places in the world. The world already has several of those kinds of books and amazing heroes. Rather, this book is about how I've successfully borrowed and adapted many strategies, tools, and lessons from my military and law enforcement leadership training, and adapted these concepts with great success during my nearly 20 years in leadership roles in the business world.

My clients asked me to write this book because they loved the Business Sergeant mentality I brought to their business problems. They thought other entrepreneurs and business leaders would appreciate my "no-nonsense, let's-get-it-done" perspective at a time when leadership and management are woefully lacking in the workplace. Because of their encouragement and support, I will now share my methods with you.

The whole point of the Business Sergeant mentality is to build a powerful and dynamic team that provides results, not excuses. The reason why people are disengaged at work is because most managers and senior leaders are generally inept at effective leadership (and can be oblivious to this fact). But when you're very intentional about the type of unit you want to create and the goals you want to reach, you can create a cohesive workforce where your staff will want to re-enlist every quarter, voluntarily and happily.

You should think of this book as a reference guide, a field manual, a handbook of field-tested best practices that you'll be referring to over and over again during the course of your entrepreneurial journey. In the military, we don't teach something to a soldier only once. We teach it to them a hundred times, so they know exactly what to do when they're in a difficult and stressful situation. They've been trained in a system and they know exactly how to put that training into action—especially when times get tough.

The best Sergeants know their job inside out. In the military, we call it being technically and tactically proficient. They lead from the front, they earn the respect of their troops, they're very approachable, and they're not afraid to get their hands dirty. They are ultimately responsible for the health and welfare of their team and the execution and success of any mission. Entrepreneurs and business leaders really need to have that kind of mindset to succeed in the business world.

Like a lot of young people, I desperately needed some discipline and accountability when I graduated from high school. And like most young men lacking direction, the military gave me the focus to harness my energy. It gave me a framework for life that empowered me to operate at a high level of excellence, rather than just trying to figure it out or wing it as I went along.

I enlisted at 17 (with Mom and Dad's signature on the age waiver). I served for nine years as an M.P. in the Army National Guard in the 34th Military Police Company, rising to the position of Squad Leader at the rank of Staff Sergeant.

During my nine-year, part-time military career in the National Guard, I became a corrections officer at a super maximum security correctional facility in Minnesota for violent felons, the worst of the worst, so to speak. Not a place where you could let your guard down, even for a minute. I learned a ton from that experience, mostly about following process to the letter, understanding and respecting other people, watching body language, "feeling" the mood or direction of the day, because if you were to misjudge a potentially dangerous situation building or disrespect the wrong person on the wrong day that could be your last day on the job or on this planet. Very high stakes on a day-to-day basis for several years of my life.

From my experience in the military and as a correctional officer, I saw the difference between Non-Commissioned Officers (Corporals to Command Sergeant Majors) and Commissioned Officers (Lieutenants to Generals) who were respected and those who were not. I prided myself on being a dedicated, squared-away leader, which is why I got my Sergeant stripes a few years early at age 21. I succeeded because I was 100% committed to be being a leader. In a business setting your troops will take their cues from your consistent day-in-and-out dedication, one of your most important priorities as a Business Sergeant.

After leaving both uniforms in 1999, I started a sales career in the home improvement industry, first selling exterior remodeling for a remodeling company. As a sales representative, I closed well over a million dollars of remodeling in each year. As a sales manager, I helped a remodeling company grow from $3 million in sales to $8 million in sales in three years, and a restoration company grow from $9 million in sales to $20 million in one year.

How did I make that happen? I was simply using the same leadership style I picked up in the Army and the Department of Corrections, and it's the same leadership style I'll be teaching you.

And, like any entrepreneur, I've also had my setbacks and failures. So, part of my success is based on having rebounded and learned from those failures, making sure they didn't repeat themselves in my future business endeavors.

During my time in the military and law enforcement, I paid close attention to my people. That was my job, because I was in leadership positions almost the whole way. I learned a ton about what makes people tick and how to get them moving in the right direction. In short, I learned how to lead and manage people in challenging, often dangerous circumstances, where there was little or no margin for error.

As a business coach, I've been able to translate those leadership lessons and teach them to other business owners and leaders. And the essence of leadership is following and carefully executing a system, day in and day out. To apply this military mindset effectively, to harness the power of this Business Sergeant attitude, you need to adopt a business operating system.

You'd be surprised at how many businesses—even large businesses that have been around for years—don't have an operating system. They don't know how to hire the right people. They don't have a vision to inspire their people. They don't have a brand that sets them apart from the crowd. They don't how to keep track of their numbers or use their sales force in the most efficient ways.

Without a system to keep you on track, it's very difficult to get better at executing. But if you apply a military-grade execution strategy at your business, you'll put together a plan that makes sense, anticipates contingencies, and ensures you have the right resources. You'll have the right people in the right seats, and everyone on your team will know precisely what their individual roles and responsibilities are. When you do that, your chances of executing to a higher standard are much, much greater.

As a business owner, everything must be systematized to make sure you're best serving your employees and clients, period. As a Business Sergeant, you must manage and interact with every aspect of your business, from where the marketing conversation begins to final execution and another referral. I've yet to see a business that can't be helped by installing a business operating system, where prioritizing and accountability are made visible and systematic. The systems I followed in uniform helped turn grey into black and white and made critical decision making easier and faster than without them. When I was helping a particularly troubled client in a turn-around of his construction business, I stumbled upon a business operating system that a peer was using with great success.

This operating system is EOS® (Entrepreneurial Operating System®), created by my now good friend Gino Wickman. Gino shows readers the entire system in his bestselling book *Traction, Get a Grip on Your Business* published by BenBella Books. After researching EOS, plus the two or three other popular business operating systems on the market, I concluded that all my clients moving forward would have to commit to an operating system, a framework, or scaffolding to help us get our arms around the whole thing. Because I felt EOS was the simplest to understand and implement, and in my opinion the most holistic, that is the one that I chose to work with.

You will read quite a few specific references to EOS (www.eosworldwide.com) in this book; keep in mind that to fully understand EOS or another operating system, you'll need to put in the time to implement the operating system purely as it was intended—not piecemeal—as the system only works optimally when you've done it correctly. While I wholeheartedly endorse this masterful system, I understand that another system might be a better fit for you, so not to be pushy or sales-y to you, I'll just refer generically to "Business Operating System" or "Operating System". You'll see just a few of the many EOS tools in action in some of the chapters, along with some simple tools that I created that dovetail with the EOS tools.

I'll also share some client stories of their experiences working with me as their EOS Implementer™. I currently spend the majority of my time teaching EOS with around 20 clients at any given time. Following the proven EOS Process™ where I get together with the leadership team for 10 full-day, off-site sessions, plus coaching as needed between those quarterly sessions over about a two-year time frame.

But first, as the team leader, you need to fortify yourself with some military-grade business logic that's going to allow you to conquer any business hill you want to assault. That's what this book is all about—to get you thinking in military terms whether or not you're part of the small percentage (around 7% of Americans) who have served, or the vast majority who have never worn a uniform.

Why is thinking in military terms so important? Because, to put it simply, business is war. Please consider the following statistics, especially if you're considering going out on your own as an entrepreneur for the first time:

- **Eight out of ten entrepreneurs who start businesses fail within the first 18 months.**[1]

- **"There is recent research by Harvard University's Shikhar Ghosh that three out of every four venture-backed firms fail."**[2]

To say that business is war is not just a statement. It's a mindset. Your competitors are literally battling you for the same dollar, and while they're not firing bullets they are firing marketing messages like commercials and online ads, they are executing sales calls with powerful sales presentations that close business and take clients off the market. How are you going to respond? How do you compete with these people on the field of business battle? It's up to you to put the right tools of business war—the right business weapons essentially—in the hands of your troops, and to make sure they know how to use them effectively.

Forbes magazine recently offered testimony to this type of approach with the following declaration: "Leadership in the 21st century requires mental

---

[1] https://www.bloomberg.com/news/articles/2002-03-03/the-bottom-line-on-startup-failures
[2] https://www.washingtonpost.com/news/fact-checker/wp/2014/01/27/do-9-out-of-10-new-businesses-fail-as-rand-paul-claims

toughness, stamina, and patience. Being a market leader demands a new breed of leadership that can withstand the punishment of the daily grind and the people pressures along the way."[3]

A Business Sergeant is exactly that kind of leader—he or she has the toughness, stamina, and patience to recruit the right troops and develop them to reach their fullest potential. I read somewhere that someone once asked legendary entrepreneur Richard Branson, "How do you motivate your best employees?" He replied, "That's easy. My very best employees are already motivated. My job is to find people who are already motivated and get the hell out of their way!"

Please note: when I say, "business is war," and make other military comparisons, I certainly don't intend to offend anyone in uniform or out of uniform. Please understand that I'm using military terminology and systems to create a foundation for your business success. I have the utmost respect for my nation's military and especially for those who have shed blood in defense of our liberties. Starting a new business or running an existing one is nothing close to the stakes you face fighting in combat for our country. Like most soldiers, I believe war is a tragedy and an absolute last resort.

Having said that, if you've ever failed badly in business (Again… most people do!) you might wish you were dead, because it's a very dark place that requires lots of soul searching, reflection, and putting the pieces back together mentally and financially to gain the confidence to take another run up that hill.

The best businesses in the world are made up of small units and teams of "A players" that use tested systems to excel in performance. You may know very little or nothing about the military, but why not learn from the U.S. military, one of the most effective team builders in the world?

The kind of Sergeant I'm talking about in this book is *NOT* a Drill Sergeant who is belittling, berating, or yelling at people. My approach is *NOT* about breaking people down to build them back up. What I'm advocating is *the mentality and mindset* of a senior unit Sergeant, a coach, a mentor, an expert with a lot of answers for your junior people. A mindset that says, "We're going to start building our highly professional team from day one, and anybody who doesn't want to be part of that team is not in the right place. We'll help you find the right unit if this one isn't right for you."

[3] http://www.glennllopis.com/online_certification/the_dangers_of_complacent_leadership

The Business Sergeant's Field Manual lays out its strategy by looking at core issues that every business leader faces, described in eleven chapters. Each chapter contains core lessons I've learned over the years, followed by a detailed look at how I worked with business clients ranging in size from $1 million to over $500 million in annual sales on the issues discussed in the chapter. Finally, I'll share some simple tools (some I've created, some are from EOS®) and action steps at the end of the chapter, which you can use immediately to put my suggestions into action.

Here's a look at how I organized this book:

CHAPTER ONE ★ Are You Committed?

As a business leader and owner who has led troops and team members, one immutable lesson has stood out for me among all others: ARE YOU COMMITTED? That's a question you'll need to ask yourself before you even think of asking it of your troops. Having a committed team will help create an environment that is both passionate and profitable for your company. But it starts with you, as a leader, having a passion for your work and complete commitment to your people.

When your team members share that same vision and drive, and you have full buy-in from your team, you've liberated the hiders and cut loose the dead weight. They see that you've made long-term decisions based on culture over profit, and that level of commitment by the owner will start to be reflected back to you by your employees.

CHAPTER TWO ★ Leadership: Are You a Leader Worth Following?

One of my favorite business quotes: "All businesses are only one leadership team away from extinction." (Author Unknown) That, in my opinion, is so true—a couple of wrong decisions and you're dead. You can't unwind it, you're just done. Just like most airplane crashes are usually the result of three or four bad decisions strung together, and not just one big mistake, going out of business also usually happens after "enough" bad calls are made.

Great leaders have an operating system and enforce accountability through consequences. Great leaders are consistent and fair, direct and decisive. Great leaders inspire and help people grow. Great leaders put their people first and park their egos at the door. Great leaders nurture talent and build the next generation of leaders who will follow in their place. Great leadership is the foundation on which all business success is built.

CHAPTER THREE ★ One Team, One Vision

Vision is all about creating that "bigger-than-ourselves" moment, because people really want to be part of something special, something larger than themselves, and being part of a winning team can be just as sweet as individual success. But if the vision is uninspiring, it will be very difficult to get anyone to follow you or to gain any traction in your business.

You need your employees to be as fired up about your passion as you are. That fire is fueled by your company's vision.

In the armed forces, a long-held credo weaves its way through every branch of service—a unit is only as strong as the person to the left or right of you. As a business owner, you want employees working for you with every fiber of their being, who are nearly as passionate and committed as you are (nobody cares as much as the people with the everything on the line...). To create that culture of reliability among your team of troops, you must start with an inspired, vivid, and shared company vision.

CHAPTER FOUR ★ How to Build a Strong Culture: Slow to Hire

Culture in the military is called *esprit de corps*. In the business world, it means defining who we are, what we do, why we do what we do, and ideally, fostering pride of the team or company we all belong to. A great culture is one where your employees will police themselves internally because they really value being part of a unit of like-minded people, and they want to protect what you have built together, because it's so valuable to them and you.

That's the mindset soldiers have: we're all in it together, all working toward the same goal of being the best. An intentional culture can inspire the same loyalty in your business and make your people *THINK BIG, GO BIG,* and ultimately *BE BIG!* They're willing to put in 100% to achieve the goal you've helped them visualize. Building that type of culture is something that takes an immense amount of effort. It begins with being very selective about who you hire. Be unrelenting in your vision to find the right people for the right seats, and to do that you have to create a culture that rests on high trust and high performance.

CHAPTER FIVE ★ Accountability: Quick to Fire

High accountability = high execution. If we're accountable to each other, if we have a culture of accountability, then when somebody says they're going to do something, it gets done. Your people are essentially putting their names, reputations, and ability to execute on the line. When we have high levels of accountability, we're not worried if your teammates will get things done if they said they would.

To build accountability, it's vital to set the bar high at the start and then *leave it there*. One of main points in this field manual is that if you stop lowering the bar, your company will start to perform at a higher level.

This involves creating an environment that's open and honest, where there's no retribution for speaking the truth. When you have a system in place for helping identify mistakes, that presents the opportunity to correct them, coach the correct response that you want, and check-ins to see if that remedial training has worked, your people won't feel bad about making mistakes, because that is how we'll all get better together. Mistakes are OK, as long as they are not repeated over and over again, so you'll need to have clear consequences for any habitual failures in performance.

CHAPTER SIX ★ Marketing and Branding

For your business to not only survive but thrive, it needs both marketing and branding. But they are NOT the same thing and are commonly confused as being so. Your brand is the key to attracting consumer interest, from how it makes them feel to buy your product, to how they talk about your brand afterwards to other potential customers when you are not around. How you market that brand and reach and engage new customers is what determines how successful your business will be—it's that simple.

Your brand is your *unique value to the world,* it's what you stand for. Your customer should clearly understand how and why you do it better than the competition, and why they need to be talking to you over your many competitors. What kind of experience will your customers have with your brand that will make customers continue to give you repeat business, and tell others about how amazing you are?

CHAPTER SEVEN ★ Sales and Sales Management

Sales are the life blood of any organization: without them, you will soon have no company. I've found that those businesses that have sales problems usually have a bunch of other problems too. Even my clients who have more sales than they know what do to with often lack an effective sales management process, which means lost business.

Often overlooked is that selling and managing sales people are two very different specialties that require very different talents. Companies will often make their top salesperson the sales manager, the wheels come off, and they wonder why. To make the distinction clear: a sales manager is somebody who spends approximately a third of their time training their sales people, another third of their time holding them accountable for the results of that training, and the last third of their time recruiting new sales people to replace those who can't meet the standard.

CHAPTER EIGHT ★ Know Your Numbers!

You may not believe this, but a lot of business owners don't really know their numbers. They just operate on gut feeling, a dangerously ignorant way to do business.

If you don't know your numbers, then you're sitting on what I call the Chaos/ Control Meter, which in business is ALWAYS ticking! If somebody's business is at 0 on the meter, they have a system in place for everything, they've automated it with technology, and a solid process is consistently followed by all. If you go up to a 10 on the scale, it means (literally) that there's a wad of cash in a desk drawer that people can grab whenever they want with little or no accounting oversight.

Most companies rank at 4 or 5 on Chaos/Control Meter. They can be functional. But to truly excel, you need financial controls, systems, policies, and procedures to make most of the chaos go away. Until then, you'll be in a kind of free-for-all where a lot of avoidable mistakes will be made. And those mistakes can be very costly.

CHAPTER NINE ★ Mission Execution (GSD)

Execution should be the expectation, not the exception to the rule. That's the bottom line: *in business, execution is paramount!* I believe vision is sold by the pound, and there's an unlimited supply of it. Great business traction or execution is sold by the carat—it's scarce and very valuable. Great business execution is rare and it takes a lot of work to achieve it. You need to commit to being great at executing, and you continue to get better at it by tracking how many of your weekly to-dos are getting ta-done.

CHAPTER TEN ★ You'll Need Some Help!

A lot of business owners have trouble letting go of control and delegating down the chain, which can have dangerous consequences. Wearing too many hats can be detrimental to your company's performance. If you make the smart move and reach out to strategic partners who are experts in their specific fields, you will prevent headaches, wasted time, inefficiency, and, most importantly, wasted money. Seeking out partners allows you to scale your business without disturbing its core, while adding complementing capacities and capabilities. You can also outsource something and see if you like it before taking it in-house.

As the Business Sergeant, remember that augmenting your forces with allies from outside the company—otherwise know in military terms as an "Attachment"—can be more efficient than training a whole new platoon of privates. By working with a network of strategic partners, you're expanding your capabilities and adding new areas of expertise that you can offer clients, as well as saving time, money, and frustration in the process.

CHAPTER ELEVEN ★ Take Care of #1

The last lesson in *The Business Sergeant's Field Manual* is also the most important: it's absolutely vital that you routinely take the focus OFF your business and put it ON your life away from the office. What is your Number one thing in life? It's usually not your business. (Even though it can feel like it if you're not careful…)

Huh? Is that really part of the military mindset? Yes, it is—it's the same philosophy that drove the military to create the concept of leave time, so soldiers could spend quality time back home with their loved ones and be reminded of what they're really fighting for.

Spending quality time with family and friends and chasing your passions outside of work keeps you and your home life healthy, and that is mission-critical to be truly healthy at work. In contrast, overworked entrepreneurs and business leaders who wear too many hats and spend too many hours at the office will suffer both personally and professionally in the long run.

***

The Business Sergeant's Field Manual is about how to gain the confidence, focus, business skill, and fortitude to transform an average business into an exceptional one. If you spend a few hours reading this book, you'll have added a single chevron (Stripe) to your arm. If you master *everything* in this book, you have a whole arm of chevrons, and people will notice those! You'll be a real Business Sergeant and will have the mindset, team, and tools to be really hard to contain. Using the approaches I suggest, you'll win a lot more on the business battlefield.

Now, let's get started!

Captain Obvious says: If you're looking to build strong leadership in your business, I highly recommend hiring a former military leader because they already get all this stuff! There are all kinds of veterans transitioning out of the military who possess extensive leadership experience.

Non-Profit programs like hireheroesusa.org and americandreamu.org, and veteran job websites like VetJobs.com and Military.com can supply you with leads. So, if you like this book's concepts and approaches, go out and hire some veterans who were great leaders in the military. They'll most likely be top performers for you, and your chances of getting to your end goal are going to be much greater than with people who haven't been tested like they have.

CHAPTER ONE

Are You Committed?

"The two most important days of your life are the day you were born and the day you find out why."

—Mark Twain

LESSON 1 ★ Are You Committed?

As a Business Sergeant, the first and most important question you need to ask yourself (before you even think of asking it of your troops) is: ARE YOU COMMITTED? In your heart of hearts, do you want to get to the top of your game so badly that you're willing to put yourself through all the pain and suffering that will be involved? Are you willing to walk onto the business battlefield day after day and fight through that pain and suffering?

You will need that kind of resilient commitment to make your vision a reality; looking for exits and for excuses to quit won't get you where you want to go. In the military, we knew our job as soldiers was to run toward the danger when everyone else was running away. It's that level of commitment that makes every branch of the U.S. military so damn effective.

You can't ask people to do stuff you're not willing to do, even if it means your own discomfort. The world needs more selfless sergeants than it does selfish ones; if you set the example, others will follow. And if you're not 100% committed to leading others, then you have no business starting a company or holding a leadership position. You should just get a job, you'll be happier and everyone around you will be happier as well.

Always remember that your employees are going to take their cues from you. If you're a leader who doesn't have the heart to cut a weak team member loose, that non-decision is going to hold back the rest of your team. In the military, you're either deployable or you're not deployable. There's no "maybe." If you're not committed, inconvenient things are going to run you off course. You'll never find the finish line, let alone cross it. By that same logic, if you're not requiring the commitment of every team, then you can't require it of any individual member.

So as a business leader, the first thing you have to ask yourself is: "Am I committed to lead other human beings? How badly do I really want this?"

In military parlance, don't dare put on the stripes if you don't care!

LESSON 2 ★ Put Passion Ahead of Profit

Another question you should ask yourself and your team every morning is: "Are you here for the passion or the profit?" The answer should be *the passion* every time.

Don't get me wrong: you want and need *both* passion and profit. But if you've just got a thirst for profit with no passion behind your idea or your work, your business won't get very far. I've found time and again with my clients that if you've got lots of passion for what you do, you'll usually have plenty of profit.

In order for your company to run at premium capacity, you need to have a shared vision with your leadership team and everyone else. How do you do that? YOU have to be excited about it, YOU have to have a mirror moment and ask yourself whether you have the same fire that you're asking your sales staff to have for the product you're selling. Even though we're all in business to make money, if you put the profit in front of your own passion, it will cost you handsomely.

I know it sounds cliché, and we've heard this time and time again in the business book world, but here it goes: would you do the job if you didn't need the money, if you were independently wealthy? If you could pick anything to do, would it be what you're doing right now? If the answer isn't yes, you probably shouldn't be doing it.

The old joke among entrepreneurs is, "Why would you want to commit to 80 hours of work a week to avoid working 40?" Ideally, the answer to this question should be, "I LOVE my business, I love my product, my customers love what we do for them, and I would never do anything else!" You need to be able to say, "I commit to this over anything else I could be committing to!"

I was working with a business owner whose company designs complex model railroad stuff. He was completely burnt out. Over the last couple years his sales had been declining, he had the wrong people in the wrong seats, and he had a bunch of people problems. In the middle of our very first session with his team it got raw, heated, and highly emotional—fresh scars, the whole deal. It was a contentious day. When I questioned him about his attitude towards his people, he was highly negative. Here he was trying to turn around his company and at the same time being really disrespectful toward his people.

I let him get it all out, and then I said, "Okay, listen, hypothetically speaking, fast-forward two months from now—your partner just bought you out, you've got a million dollars for conversation's sake, what are you going to go do?"

"I'd go design train stuff," he replied.

"Well, isn't that what you do now?" I responded. "You already have market share. Why would you want to start over on your own instead of making some people changes, changing your outlook, and bringing some happiness back into your life? Because if you're going to sell your business at a big discount and then go back to doing exactly what you're doing now, you would effectively be lighting quite a bit of your time, money, and effort on fire. The problem is not about your passion for what you do."

That was a lightning bolt moment for him. He had to admit it made no sense, and he came around. I got him to see that he was unhappy with how things were running in his business, but not with the business itself. Once we turned the mirror back on him, the rest of the afternoon had a completely different flavor. Once he understood the problem wasn't about his passion, that instead it was about his "failure in leadership" (his words!), we were able to start exploring that attitude with the rest of his staff. We were able to make the changes necessary to get everyone on the same set of tracks, in pursuit of the same shared vision. So the big lesson we all learned there was to stay connected with the passion and to make sure it was shared by everyone in the company.

There are really only a few ways to participate in business: either you come up with a vision you're passionate about, you commit to it with everything you've got, and you recruit like-minded people who have the same passion and excitement, OR, you find an attractive vision that you share as if it was your own. If you're not in a position to do your own thing, and most people are not, at a minimum please get out of the rat race and find something with similar or better compensation that you're much more passionate about. Sometimes people choose a lower paying but much more satisfying career, because they put a high value on their happiness over material goods that a big gig can provide.

A third option, which I believe many people follow (Remember; in 2016 Gallop reported that 70% of the Millennial U.S. workforce is "disengaged"[4]), is to not have any passion in your work and save it for your home life—whether you like to work on cars or ride mountain bikes or ski with your kids. Millions of American workers have become 9 to 5 drones who just hit the "go to work" button and drink five or six cups of coffee as they grind their way through the day. Then they spend their personal time chasing the passions that energize them, and their work is just a means to live that life.

Think about that for a minute... You spend a third of your life asleep, a third of your life chasing your passions outside of work, and a third working. If you are not having fun, being challenged, or feeling fulfilled at work that is a huge chunk (50%) of the waking hours of your life where you have to be somewhere you don't want to be. How free do you feel under that scenario? I'd argue not very... and I believe that is a shame. In a free society workers can choose their vocation and their workplace vs. being told what to do by their government. How many people actually exercise that right? We've all heard that freedom isn't free, as many brave veterans have paid a very steep price for our freedom. Being free isn't just about your ability to choose your vocation and workplace, I believe it's about choosing to live the life you want vs. the life you have. Have you ever seen the photo or video of an ant that won't cross a circled line drawn around it on a table because it thought that was a real barrier?

I've met lots of people that for whatever reason have opted not to be free. I hope you're not one of them, because at the end of the day all the ant has to do is press forward to be free.

Another way of telling the difference between a passion and an interest is this: if you're interested in something, you'll pursue it until some adversity comes around, and then you'll drop it when its expedient to do so.

But if you're passionate about doing that same thing, it doesn't matter what gets in your way, you're still going to forge ahead and do it. You're willing to deal with the adversity because your passion is greater than any adversity.

You can't be *interested* in building a great business culture; you have to be

 [4] http://www.gallup.com/businessjournal/195209/few-millennials-engaged-work.aspx

passionate about it, along with everyone who works with you. As the business owner or leader, you have to understand that without an inspiring central vision and clear core values that you will defend and enforce passionately, you'll find it very difficult to inspire anyone to feel fanatically committed to you, your company, or your customers.

Passion comes from your "personal why" and that of your team members as well. What are you truly passionate about? Do you really want this, or do you just *think* you should really want this? Ask that of your team and make sure they ask it of themselves.

We have a long-held philosophy in the military that we're only as strong as our weakest link. Sage wisdom, right? I realize it's the world's most overused cliché, but that doesn't stop it from being 100% true. It's as true in business as in a military unit, and that means that business owners and leaders— especially a small business owners and leaders—must be consistently asking of their employees: *Are you really all-in or not?*

If you go into battle half-committed, you're likely to become a casualty, or worse, you'll cause someone else to become one; it's the same in business. In order for your business to sustain itself, the owner and their leaders have to be 100% in, all the way, no hesitation. If you don't have passion, you're going to crush your people's hopes and dreams and waste years of their lives (and your own). So when you do choose a business, choose wisely and then commit fully!

LESSON 3 ★ Be Committed to Your Employees

I have a personal theory that if 70% of Americans are disengaged at work it's because 70% have managers that are not committed to them and aren't developing them. Employees feel disengaged when their managers aren't investing in them, or are unappreciative or steal credit from them. I could go on and on about everything I've seen related to this topic. The root of this problem is that the majority of employers are not committed to their employees as their #1 priority. I often see employees placed well behind profit, shareholders, customers, and sometimes even vendors, and I believe that is a HUGE mistake, because without your team you have no business.

In fact, I'd be willing to bet that the disengagement numbers are higher on the management side than on the employee side. That's because the passion just isn't there. People want to have some meaning in their professional lives;

they don't just want to churn out T.P.S. reports all day. Most of the companies I work with need lots of help in raising engagement in all departments. The problem is systemic.

Disengagement should be a slap in the face of any business leader. If you're not committed to developing and investing in people, you'll lose money and opportunity in the marketplace. When work looks like it's getting done but isn't really getting done to the correct standard, the cost of that lack of commitment is substantial in both time and money.

The best leaders are always thinking: "What can I do for you today to make you a happier, healthier, and more engaged member of our team?"

When I was a sergeant, I routinely asked the men and women whom I was responsible for what I call forward-thinking questions: "Where do you want to be in a year?" and "Are you currently challenged?" The bottom line is: great leaders inspire and help people grow. They never assume anything, and so in business, on a quarterly basis, we need to sit down with our people and have that conversation. Great leaders take an interest in their team members and inspire them to take extra steps to grow, whether in means learning new job skills, getting additional education or certifications, or learning a foreign language. There's a great meme on business social media that I like to quote: the CFO of a company says to their CEO, "Hey, what if we invest in these people and then they leave us?" The CEO replies, "Well, what if we don't and they stay?"

Conversely, when you invest in your team, you create a work force that is highly committed to concepts like quality and accuracy, and your business is a lot more profitable and fun to be around. Business owners don't always understand how quickly you can be out of business if clients aren't coming back for a second visit because of a first bad experience. You can find yourself spending more and more on marketing to make up for that deficit, and at the same time losing more and more people out the back door until eventually the math is no longer sustainable. You're dead in business battle, a.k.a., a business casualty.

Remember, there are a lot of people who offer whatever you're offering. What separates the exceptional companies from the herd is that their leaders are absolutely committed to their employees, investing in their growth and development, and motivating them to consistently execute at a high level to ensure customer satisfaction.

As soon as your employees sense or see that "this person doesn't care about me," that's the moment they no longer care about you, your company, your profit margins, your customers, or your reputation. That's the spillover effect that trickles down into the attitudes of employees.

They don't have strong leadership keeping them engaged, motivated, passionate, and 100% committed.

LESSON 4 ★ Learn How to Assess and Monitor Commitment

I can walk into any company for the first time and, in usually within five minutes, from the atmosphere and mood know if it's a super healthy culture, an average one, or an unhealthy one. You can tell when someone would rather be getting a root canal than talking about their core values or what they are accountable for.

Usually, about 50% of offices are in the "average" category—not terrible, not great. About twenty percent are "wow." I really like the look and feel of the place. I can feel the energy and it's really positive. They seem to be on to something here. And then about 30% are clearly not doing very well. People have their heads down working. There's not much going on. There's a lack of personalization and individuality in the workplace. Lots of drawn circles holding them back.

It's important for you, as the leader, to assess and monitor the commitment of your people. This is not a gray area, but black and white. You can feel someone's commitment through their personal energy. Do they look like they *want* to be here, or do they look like they *have* to be here? Your people should be so passionate and committed to the company's mission that you have to pry them off the mountain when it's getting dark and tell them to go home.

It's pretty easy to tell who has energy and who does not. Start having conversations about the future with your employees, or what I call "dreaming with my employees." Ask them: "What would you like to do in the future?" or "Where would you like to be in two or three years?" In my experience, people who have a lack of vision for themselves or for their role in the business have already checked out. These are the employees who are "kinda" committed.

As a military police sergeant and as a corrections sergeant, I learned the art of asking questions, and this can be a good technique for testing someone's passion about anything. Ask three or four successive questions about what they love most. Usually if people are faking—after the first or second question you'll be able to spot whether or not they're getting creative on the spot.

When you're asking somebody what they're really passionate about and they say skiing, you might say, "Oh really, what kind of skis do you have?" They give you an answer. Then you ask them, "When was the last time you went skiing for a whole day?" If they say "two years ago," you know they're not all that passionate about skiing. Really passionate and committed people usually find a way to tap into that passion.

This fakery happens all the time, especially in the workplace. Ask someone about their work responsibilities or a company product. I'll say, "I'm a new client. Explain this product to me in thirty seconds. Why should I want this product?"

If they say, "Well, it's a good product, it's better than the last one, it costs a little less, it's a little lighter, it's got a little bit more memory," if they're just reciting factual data, that means that they know their product but they're just regurgitating the specs.

But if somebody says, "Oh my God, you're not going to believe this thing. It totally crushes the last model. Listen to what this thing will do for you." They start talking about the features, the advantages, the benefits, how it's going to save me time, how this product is the best, nothing can compete with it. There's a sparkle in their eye that they can't fake.

If someone's really committed, they'll share their level of commitment with you and the passion behind it, whether you ask them about their "personal why" or one of your products. It's key that you and your team are equally all-in.

You can't be half-pregnant, but in business it's rarely that clear. Usually we're dealing with lots of shades of gray, and that's why we need to bring military-grade clarity into the workplace. The bottom line is the same: you're either committed to the mission or you're not committed to the mission. It's very dangerous for everybody involved when it "kinda" looks like it's getting done but it's not really getting done.

LESSON 5 ★ The 90-Day Commitment Review

You may be thinking, "Wow, the commitment mentality sounds great but my team will never go for it!" The simplest way to overcome that fear is by facing it in front of them, by giving everyone an opportunity to reenlist or to decide your company isn't for them. I first learned this concept from Zappos CEO Tony Hsieh. Zappos puts new hires through a paid training class, then offers a substantial (relative to their base pay) buyout to trainees to leave. This is to weed out the ones who aren't passionate about working at Zappos and providing the legendary customer care Zappos is known for. They are the ones who just want money, so they take it and move on. I like to call those types *mercenaries*. I think we all get the idea what happens when a better opportunity comes along for those types.

Your people should essentially re-enlist not every year, but every quarter. Every 90 days, ask your people, "Are you going to re-enlist or take a walk?" If it's the latter, offer them some easy money and a nice recommendation letter. It sounds harsh perhaps, but if you offer this every quarter and some people take the buyout, that's a beautiful thing in my eyes. Because they've essentially said, "I don't want to be in your squad anymore." You can help them make a transition and you're free to find staff members who really want to be on your team. The person leaving wins, you, your existing employees and your company win, your new employee wins, and ultimately your customers win.

It's time to implement a key tool called the Quarterly Re-enlistment Questionnaire (found at the end of the chapter), which will give you real-time feedback on your team's commitment and helps keep expectations crystal clear for all parties involved. This questionnaire allows your employees to share both positive and negative feedback. What I've learned is that people don't quit bad companies, they quit bad managers. This is a chance to find out what your team thinks about your company's management skills and to make changes in your leadership based on their feedback.

Your company will run far more efficiently when you have 100% commitment from your employees, and for those who aren't giving it, you'll know how to make the necessary course corrections to make sure you have commitment going forward from everyone on your team!

I love the idea that you're either all the way in or you're out the door. If it's the latter, that's okay, we still care for you and we won't leave you on the side of the road. But if they really don't want this and decide not to reenlist, they're saving you a lot of money and making your team a stronger one in the long run. You're not keeping someone who's uncommitted and holding back you and their co-workers.

In my experience at higher performing businesses, for every ten people, seven are going to be committed to the job and three are not, and those three need to be the first to go. You can then replace them with three people who want to be in those seats and are looking for that kind of a unit. Yes, even high performing companies aren't perfect tens all around, those businesses that have 10 out of 10 are truly "Elite" businesses and they are very rare, and they can do whatever they want to because of all of those "A" players on their roster.

"The military will almost always give you a second chance if you fail to meet a course's standards, but what they never do is lower the standard."

So I encourage a quarterly commitment meeting with your people where you can make sure you have an all-volunteer, highly motivated, highly dedicated, 100% committed force to take into business battle every day. The military will almost always give you a second chance if you fail to meet a course's standards, but what they never do is lower the standard. You and your leadership team need to commit to keeping the standards high and holding everyone accountable to them. One thing I heard in the military over and over was, "The more we sweat in peacetime, the less we bleed in war." Again, it all starts with commitment.

Always remember that the weak links in a chain always start with the leader. Make the tough calls so you can move down the field with a stronger team. That will be a central call to action throughout this book—step up into the reality of commitment and BE A STRONG LEADER!

FOCUS ON THE CLIENT
Solving a Commitment Problem at 303 Software

In my first meeting with Matt Jaffe and his partner Stefan Ramsbott's company, 303 Software, everyone looked visibly shaken. Their software development shop was in horrible shape. There was a culture-first over revenue-first approach to the business. The sales pipeline had emptied. They only had a couple of projects to work on and several active projects were over budget. They were unable to make payroll without getting a personal loan.

Matt and Stefan had started another venture a year prior that required Matt's focus had gone away from their core business at 303 Software. While their focus was on building success in their new product venture, 303 Software had little or no commitment or accountability in Matt's absence.

Some of the software developers were coming in the crack of 11 a.m. and leaving at 2 or 3 p.m. There were video game breaks at lunch that extended past the hour. They were picking and choosing what projects they wanted to work on. Anything that was really difficult or challenging was the new guy's problem. People were taking way too much time off, like 60, 70 days a year or more.

There wasn't a lot of commitment in evidence while Matt was gone. His lack of commitment to leading the company while he and Stefan began pursuing another venture had infested the entire organization.

The first step was to get them to see how bad the company really was. The second step was to determine who was really with them and worth saving—who wanted to leave and who wanted to stay because they believed the company was worth saving.

Let's have Matt tell the story from here:

We're software developers, by nature we're problem solvers, and we think that if we can't solve the problem, then nobody else can. So it took me quite a bit of politicking and lobbying to get my team on board with the idea that we needed help, that we weren't going to solve the problems ourselves, and that we needed to make a big change. This was a 10-year-old company, and although I was still the owner, we'd launched another business about two years ago that I left to run the development team there as the full-time CTO. I had been head-down on this new start-up, and hadn't paid enough attention to what was happening at 303 Software. Everyone was doing whatever they felt like doing; people were setting their own hours. There was no management, accountability, communication, or ability to measure things objectively.

We had a really tough meeting where Chris introduced his "No B.S." approach, and that was what we needed because a lot of the team here was in denial. We didn't need to talk about feelings and interpersonal relationships. We needed to execute on something quickly, and Chris' no-nonsense style—"Here's the reality, now deal with it," was exactly what we needed. He asked really penetrating questions that made the executive team get a little defensive, until one person got very real and honest about everything we had been avoiding. That person pointed out the huge failures and gaps in what we were doing, and from that point on the meeting changed. We realized that we needed help in keeping the team honest and focused on the problems in front of us that weren't being addressed.

Chris put our numbers on the board and said, "You guys are basically screwed right now. You're in a terrible situation, on the brink of going out of business." Nobody but me had been saying that up to that point. Until that first meeting with Chris, people were still papering over the problems, being Pollyannaish, and not really facing the truth. But once we'd sat down with Chris, his temperament, personality, and ability to cut through all the B.S. helped us admit and confront the magnitude of the problems we were facing.

We had hired a sales executive who turned to be a really good salesman in terms of what he said he could do for the company, but in executing did absolutely nothing. He showed up for one of our coaching meetings 20 minutes late and Chris dressed him down in front of the whole team. That moment was a turning point for us. That was exactly the kind of straight talk we needed at the company. The sales executive didn't take any responsibility; he later complained about how mean Chris was. We decided to let him go. Chris showed us how to cut the cords rather than hang onto people and it made the company much better.

After everyone was no longer in denial about how dire the situation was, they knew some really big sacrifices had to be made. They had a much larger staff than they needed and, after further digging, I found that a good portion of these people either weren't living up to their potential or were actually quite toxic to the business. Matt was still hesitant to let anyone go even though their very survival was at stake. I told him that they were going to have to let go of four or five people in the next week or the company would be going out of business in the next month. That's how serious it was.

They followed my advice and that began the company's turnaround. Here's Matt again:

> When we started working with Chris, we adopted a formal structure to evaluate whether we needed to make a hire. We didn't have that before. We also instituted checkpoints and deliverables for every quarter; now we know if somebody's actually executing on what they say they're doing. This made it very easy to see that our sales guy wasn't performing because we could evaluate him in terms of our criteria and values. When it came time to deliver the quarterly "rocks," which are big targets that Chris helped us identify, he also fell short. Before we worked with Chris, we would have muddled around and had circular conversations and not been able to come to a decision about letting him go because we didn't have the criteria to make a decision.
>
> That was something huge Chris introduced into the company culture: evaluating if we have the right person in the right seat, if that person is adhering to the values of the company, and if that person is delivering. Now, thanks to EOS®, we have a system for holding them accountable for their work, which we never had in the past. Now everybody at the company is working in the same headspace.
>
> Between Chris's coaching style and the EOS(R) system we have become really good at not making personnel decisions personal. If somebody's not happy here, it's a lot easier for us to say, "You're not happy, we're not happy, you should be happy and find that happiness somewhere else."

Today, a year later, 303 Software is a transformed and revitalized company. About a third of the company was comprised of a core of people who thought the company was special, that it could be saved and needed to be saved. That core stuck with the company through its transformation and is still there. They've turned over a large part of the company except for the owners and those core employees.

The number of employees is actually pretty similar to a year ago, but instead of having a twenty C and D players, they now have twenty A and B players.

They've completely restructured their sales funnel. Now they've got a successful demand generation program running. They have a new government contracting division to do business with the world's largest client. They have made changes in every part of their business.

The problems that plagued 303 Software in the past can never happen again due to the controls we've established. The company now engages its employees. Every week they take a confidential survey that allows them to speak more candidly without fear of retribution.

A crisis that began with an uncommitted leadership team has been resolved by a renewal of commitment, from the top down.

"PULLING THE TRIGGER" GO/NO-GO DECISION WORKSHEET

Can we/Should we commit our team to this?

1. What are we considering? _____

2. Why are we considering it? _____

3. What happens if we don't commit? _____

4. What happens if we do commit? _____

5. Do we have the expertise? _____

6. Do we have the budget? _____

7. Who is going to "own" the decision? _____

8. Who is going to "own" the execution? _____

9. Margin/Complexity compared to our average? _____

10. Is demand High/Medium/Low _____

11. Can we scale it? _____

12. Our level of commitment vs. existing proven products or services
High / Medium / Low _____

─ OUTCOMES ─

If _____ happens (positive) we will do _____

If _____ happens (negative) we will do _____

We will review this decision on (date) _____ / _____ / _____

QUARTERLY RE-ENLISTMENT QUESTIONNAIRE

Make it clear that employees must share positive and negative feedback from the last 90 days.

—— Answer from 1 to 10, with 10 being highest level of satisfaction. ——

1. Rate your overall satisfaction with this unit. _____

2. If the best place you've ever worked is a 10, how do you rate your current company? _____

3. How well does your leader do supporting and developing you? (time, tools, training) _____

4. How well does your leader hold you accountable? _____

5. How well does your leader hold others accountable? _____

6. How well does your leader communicate with you? _____

7. How likely are you to recommend your company to a friend who is looking for work? _____

8. Rate the team health (unit cohesion) on your team? _____
   At the whole company? _____

9. Do you feel adequately recognized for your contributions to the unit? _____

10. How likely are you to seek advancement within the company? _____

—— In addition, answer the following questions: ——

Why do you work here vs. somewhere else? _____

_____

_____

_____

What is your dream assignment within this organization? _____

_____

_____

_____

What skills are you willing to pick up to climb and grow? _____

_____

_____

_____

"Are you enlisting for another quarter of service, or would you like to take the buyout today?" _____

_____

_____

_____

For any answers under an 8, ask for more detail. Ask for feedback and suggestions that would bring the number up.

Then ask the employee to commit to another 90 days of service to the company, with you serving them as their leader. If they decline, offer 45 days severance to offload.

CHAPTER TWO

Are You a Leader Worth Following?

"The day your soldiers stop bringing you their problems is the last day you stopped leading them. They have either lost confidence that you can help them or concluded that you do not care.

Either is a failure of leadership." **—General Colin Powell**

"Only three **things happen naturally** in organizations: friction, confusion, and underperformance. **Everything else requires leadership.**"

—Peter Drucker

The U.S. Army's Leadership Field Manual has three main points that are a direct corollary to being a strong Business Sergeant who is able to lead a strong team of troops: *BE, KNOW,* and *DO.*

BE of high moral character.

KNOW your specialty.

And to *DO* means not being a theorist with a desk growing out of your chest, but rather leading from the front and setting a great example for the rest of the team to follow. Leadership is about setting a vision and management is about executing that vision and managing the accountability that goes along with it.

Most people can pretty easily articulate why they enjoy working for a strong leader.

"He always listens to me."

"She makes us feel like a team."

"She doesn't steal credit. I was in a presentation with my boss, and she recognized me to her superiors for my contributions and ideas."

These types of leaders make it very easy for their team members to want to give 100%. Andrew Carnegie once said, "no man will make a great leader who wants to do it all himself, or to get all the credit for doing it."

The Army also has some key leadership values that are directly applicable here: *LOYALTY, DUTY, RESPECT, SELFLESS SERVICE, HONOR, INTEGRITY,* and *PERSONAL COURAGE.*

There's a saying from the Army's leadership manual that goes like this: "Leadership is not about rank or time in the uniform, but about responsibility, accountability, and execution of the mission."

But are most business leaders following these principles and incorporating them into their day-to-day responsibilities? Consider these statistics:

- *Harvard Business Review:* "Executives at the companies we surveyed spent an average of 21 hours a month together in leadership team meetings."[5]

- *Forbes:* "78% of leaders have difficulty understanding and effectively articulating the requirements to thrive in the rapidly changing marketplace—and the consequences of not doing so. Perhaps this explains why only 32% of leaders define themselves as change agents."[6]

- The esteemed Brandon Hall Group's 2015 State of Leadership Development Study reports that while "leadership development earns a top spot year after year after year on organizations' talent priority lists, 36% do not have a formal leadership development strategy."[7]

- Training Mag.com: **"Leadership shortfalls are, and will continue to prove to be, the single greatest differentiator between high-performance and all other organizations."**[8]

[5] https://hbr.org/2004/09/stop-wasting-valuable-time
[6] https://www.forbes.com/sites/glennllopis/2015/07/16/four-reasons-leaders-are-too-afraid-of-making-the-wrong-decisions
[7] https://trainingmag.com/study-shows-leadership-development-rated-below-average-or-poor-more-one-third-organizations
[8] ibid.

The number one reason, in my view, that people are disengaged is that they're being let down by poor leadership, constantly disappointed and confused by the people "in charge". After a while they just shut off. People don't feel like they're heard, that they don't have a voice in the process. It's pretty easy to get disengaged when you realize you have no control, that whether you care or don't care the effect is the same. People want to see that their inputs directly affect the outputs of their work.

Disengagement is also a result of a lack of an open, honest environment. People are afraid to stick their necks out because they either have taken a chance on something they believed in, or they witnessed another attempt by someone else that didn't end well for them. They've got a couple of kids in college, so they're just going to play it safe and go along with everything the boss says, whether it makes sense or not.

Your troops will feel honored to be led by a great and strong leader (too often the exception to the rule). Really, really strong leaders—the kind of person you'll follow anywhere—are very rare. Leadership isn't something we do when we feel like it. It's something that surrounds us like the Force. I find that the best leaders don't just lead at work, they lead at home, and in their community, because they just can't help it, it's who they are. You have to come into the office every morning and ask yourself, "How can I lead these people to greatness today? They want to be led, but can I do it, and am I willing to do it?"

LESSON 6 ★ Strong Leaders Have an Operating System

The first step in demonstrating strong leadership is to pick an operating system, commit to it, and then follow it religiously. That may seem obvious, but I've seen numerous businesses operate without any system—303 Software, which you read about in the last chapter, was just one of them. Without the intentionality a system brings, people will slide back into their normal human behaviors and then you're back to getting inconsistent results. If for some reason your people are having a good week, you'll get a ton of results; if they aren't inspired to work hard the following week, you'll most likely get much less. Who's running this business?

But if you're using a system, you will have consistent output; any time performance falls below the standard you've established, the system will indicate it and allow you to fix it. The responsiveness of the system allows you to be more agile and more flexible than if you don't have one. Without one, you're basically searching around half the day figuring out what's broken. With a system, you immediately know what's broken and can fix it immediately.

The lack of a process leads to a lack of confidence and control. You can't have control if you've never really instilled in your people what the expectations are: "This is what we expect you to do it, here are the guidelines…" You'd be surprised how many leaders haven't had those basic, one-on-one discussions. The employee thinks she knows what you want and expect, but if you don't clearly define expectations, mission, and tasks at the start, and enforce them in a consistent way, you're not being a Business Sergeant.

This goes back to the BE/KNOW/DO philosophy: When you really know your stuff, confidence comes from the repetition of executing successfully. If you don't have an operating system that will raise flags when something is amiss, it's very difficult to foster a culture of consistent execution. If you are simply unaware, it's very easy for you to become comfortable with average levels of execution. That level of performance eventually becomes normal and accepted, sinking into the organization's fabric. And that can cause problems.

I point to one of my favorite quotes: "All businesses are only one leadership team away from extinction." Whoever said that nailed it in my opinion, because a couple of wrong decisions and you're dead. You can't unwind it, you're just done.

LESSON 7 ★ A Strong Leader Enforces Accountability Through Consequences

When I begin coaching a business, I'll ask people, "On a scale of 1–10, what level of accountability exists in your organization?"

The average number that I get is 3. I often find a great disparity between how the leadership team and the business owner rate accountability. The leadership team will usually give accountability a 6 or a 7, but the owner will rate it a 3. The owner's accountability rating is almost always several points below the staff's rating. It's almost as if the owner is passive-aggressively saying, "I wish you all would be a little more accountable to me and each other."

When you have a scorecard tracking everyone's weekly activities, you're either "on track" this week—thumbs up, high-fives, great job—or you're "off track", and it's time to, "put this on the issues list and discuss what's not working."

That's the kind of black-and-white leadership and accountability that exists in the military, but unfortunately there's a lot of gray areas in the business world. It needs to be black and white. When you have agreed-upon and communicated expectations, they're either met or they're not met. There's no ambiguity. Expectations need to be shared by each communicator—instead of belonging to one person and the rest working on assumptions— then concrete agreements need to be made with each other to ensure clarity and accountability. There is specific agreement about what constitutes the completion of a task to the agreed-upon standard.

Therefore, as a leader, you need to establish really high levels of accountability: "If this doesn't happen, what happens as a consequence?" I usually see a lot of barking by the owner, but they usually don't have very sharp teeth. They make a lot of noise but nothing really happens because there are no real consequences. There's no scar, no reminder, no lesson to be learned.

So as a Business Sergeant, establish consequences with your team: "If this is what happens, this is the recourse." When you have a set of rules and guidelines, and there are clear and universal consequences for breaking them, you'll find that tasks get accomplished on a much more regular basis. I like to give the example: If everyone always got a warning for speeding instead of a speeding ticket (a big fine, increased insurance premium, points lost on your driver's license etc.) people would speed a lot more than they already do. I know I would.

When leadership is setting general guidelines for the bare minimum performance, when "it's all good" as long as no one commits a felony, a passive, lazy culture will infest your company. When a new leader walks into an environment like that, it's extremely challenging to effect change. Because everyone's been left to their own prioritizing with little central leadership, numerous fiefdoms and political complexities will have developed. The wrong kind of employees will get used to this climate as no or low accountability works great for folks who like to screw off all day on your dollar. When it comes time to change that behavior to a healthier more productive one, prepare for a fight; they will resist, so you'll have to dig in and stay committed to your end state.

A strong leader has a strong central message, a set of well-defined core values, a crystal-clear business focus, and the ability to create and inspire the team to line up behind the goals.

Keeping the wrong people in the wrong positions for too long can tie a knot in your business operations that will be very hard to untie. That's why you might just want to cut the cord and move forward without all that unnecessary complexity.

In fact, I've been part of an entire FLUSH of a leadership or management team, where a whole department gets purged, when we've determined the problem is just so bad that we can't fix it. In those cases, the organization was rebuilt on the foundation of the vision, core values and principles we've been talking about, and with much greater success.

We'll go into detail about accountability in Chapter 5.

LESSON 8 ★ Strong Leaders Are Firm, Fair and Consistent

The concept of being firm, fair, and consistent was first taught to me in the Department of Corrections when I was just 20 years old. That's how we were told to carry ourselves to enforce the many rules of the prison, and that's also how you could expect to be led by your Sergeant. In a place like that the price to pay for inconsistent, unclear, or weak leadership was very steep indeed.

Firm: Be clear and direct about your expectations. Be confident in your delivery.

Fair: Treat everyone in the exact same way you'd like to be treated.

Consistent: No one wants a Jekyll and Hyde character as their boss.

If you're not firm, fair, and consistent, you create way too much extra work for your subordinates—and yourself.

We've been talking about how to be firm and fair up until now. Being consistent might be the toughest part. Being consistent as a leader means being consistent with your attitude first and foremost: when your troops walk into a leadership team meeting in the morning, they shouldn't be asking: "Which leader do you think we're going to get today? The fun, motivated one? Or the bossy one who's pissed at the world?" You can't be the Dr. Jekyll and Mr. Hyde kind of leader who is all too common. As leaders, we can't have two or three alter egos. Just as you're asking your people to leave their personal issues at the door, you, as their leader, need to be the first to do the same on a daily basis, no matter what kind of mood you're in.

We must be consistent. Consistent in our actions, our mannerisms. Consistent with our enforcement of the standards. Making expectations simple and easy to understand is an important tenet of business leadership. Everyone's head has to be in the same game, and clear, consistent leadership can get you there the quickest. We shouldn't treat one group or one person differently than anyone else. Not only can that get you into big trouble, HR-wise, it's just really unclear to people. Even if you're not trying to make favorites or gain favors, that's how it appears. In this case, perception is reality.

Consistent leadership means staying positive, focused, committed, and putting in 100%, without letting whatever is going on with you personally—good or bad—get in the way. This is where good management comes into play: making deadlines on time, keeping a finger on the pulse of your team's enthusiasm for the mission, and helping them execute by leading through example.

When I work with leadership teams, one of my favorite questions to ask is, "What about your reputation as a leader?" The point I try to drill home is that leadership is not all about the rank; it's about the troops' respect! In the military, I met a lot of non-commissioned and commissioned officers who earned a very high rank but they hadn't earned respect. They got their required salutes and "yes sirs," but as soon as they left the room everyone ripped into them. It was sobering to see someone who held rank and authority who thought they had the mettle to lead, but who didn't really have any respect from their people. If you're going to be an effective leader, you MUST have the respect of ALL of your troops, not just some of them. They will follow your lead if they respect you as a leader, and that respect comes from clear and consistent leadership.

LESSON 9 ★ A Strong Leader is Direct and Decisive

It hurts in the long run if you can't be direct with your people about what they need to do and what needs to be changed. Candy-coating problems doesn't fix them. You need to be able to say to people, "We have a problem and we will fix it."

Your employee might push back and think you're being too harsh, but I'd rather have that type of response than the passive-aggressive kind: "Don't worry, that's fine, I'll take care of it." That employee is likely to badmouth you the moment you leave the room, and that type of behavior only chips away at the company's culture. A passive-aggressive, complacent environment is pervasive in the business world, poisoning good will and dragging down office morale.

At the end of the day, you need to be firm with your people and stand for what you believe in—and what *everyone* agreed they were going to believe in—the core values. Be clear: "This is how we operate as a company; if you don't like it, we'll still love you, but you'll have to go work somewhere else."

A lot of people would say that an ultimatum like that is too direct, but when you're direct you don't waste any time. Being brutally honest will save you a load of time and energy, which you can spend on tasks that are more productive for you and your company. You're actually doing everyone a favor when you say what needs to be said rather than tip-toeing around the problem.

That said, a good Business Sergeant does NOT mean putting on the round, brown hat and screaming like a crazy person at your troops. That's a DRILL Sergeant, and the two shouldn't get confused—especially if you're preparing to step into that role for the first time as a business owner. A Drill Sergeant trains and indoctrinates new soldiers; our approach here is NOT to do that in quite the same intense way because it can turn your troops off before they even commit. In the corporate setting, it's absolutely correct that on sensitive topics you should, "praise in public and admonish in private."

So be assertive and be bold, but don't be coarse and unprofessional. *This is what I want you to do—now go do it,"* isn't the best way to lead. Even when you're firing someone, you can do it in a kind way, while remaining firm and direct in cutting the cord. Even if it makes you the bad guy temporarily, your committed troops will respect and love you for it in the long run. Remember, no one likes carrying dead weight, no matter where they sit in the chain of command.

The beautiful thing about the military is that they'll tell you when you screw up. They're upfront and direct because lives depend on it. But in the day-to-day operation of your business, you have to do the same thing—call it out in the open in a respectful way, especially on the little stuff, because I think it brings awareness to those issues that can't be achieved in private one-on-meetings. If I have ten people in the room and one of them made a minor mistake, I'll call them out on it in a respectful manner, and then end with, "thumbs up, we're good? Thank you." This becomes a lesson for everyone, not just the person I called out, and that will accelerate the learning curve at your company. Just make sure that it's a little thing and not a major issue that needs to be discussed privately.

I'm a big believer in saying to people, "Listen, if I call you out in a public setting, you're just going to have to be okay with that, we can all learn from mistakes, mistakes are ok, it's how we respond, how we recover." And by the way, when you do that, those mistakes rarely happen a second or third time. You have to be a little tough sometimes, but it's for everyone's benefit—especially your own.

Strong leaders are also decisive—they sometimes make decisions before they have all the information they need. We can't always wait for the true indicators to come in before we pivot on something; business is never that clear, and that's where strong leadership and great relationships on a team come into play. A decision has been made and people trust in who they're following. In contrast, a weak leader will fumble in finding solutions to problems, leading to weak consensus management and lots of "paralysis by analysis". No team will have confidence in that type of leader.

LESSON 10 ★ Leaders Eat Last

We have a rule in the military that *Leaders Eat Last,* and it's not meant metaphorically. Sergeants don't eat until their whole platoon has been fed. Instead of eating, they check on the health and welfare of their troops, joke with them a little bit, and thank them for their hard work. It's an opportunity to lead by letting the team go first, and I think doing that three times a day really shows everyone how "Servant" leadership should look like.

I've even seen times the mess hall has run out of hot chow before the Sergeants get to eat, and they'll be sitting there eating an MRE (Meal Ready to Eat in an air-sealed package). Their troops will sometimes offer to share their hot food (or they'll just point and laugh, because they're pretty happy anytime they're not getting the short end of the stick). It's a great feeling for a leader when the team knows that they come before you do.

Selfless leaders ask: "What can I do to make you better? What can I do to make you faster, stronger, and more prepared for the challenges you face? What knowledge, support and tools do you need from me?"

When a leader has invested in his people time and time again, it's a lot easier for that leader to ask 100% from his team. They'll say, "Absolutely, I'll follow you anywhere." They're returning the favor. Versus an uninterested, uninvolved, and uncommitted leader, who might get away with putting in half a workday and is oblivious to the effect that has on his team. In the long run, no company or department can survive when it's commanded by a stuffed shirt who doesn't inspire professional growth among his team, and who doesn't put the same investment into the vision and mission as his team members.

The real leader—the well-respected and *inspirational* one—is someone people really want to get behind. People enjoy being part of the professional working environment that kind of leader creates, where there's open communication and team members are allowed to share their opinions, both positive and negative, without fear of retribution or favor. It's a helluva lot more fun to a member of that type of team.

LESSON 11 ★ Ownership Is Not Leadership

Another concept I try to drive home with clients is Ownership vs. Leadership. There is a *HUGE* difference between the two! Just because you're an owner or a family relation of the owner, you're not entitled to be a leader. Leadership positions should be *earned* positions. You really do have to earn your stripes. You have to make sure those family members in leadership positions have as much knowledge and experience as those non-relatives who earned it the old-fashioned way.

In the small business universe, we have what's called an "owner's box" and an "ownership unit." Too often, those owners weren't good leaders inside the company and pulled what I like to call "owner's crap." And it was *not cool*.

Being the owner doesn't allow you to violate your values or behave in a manner that wouldn't be tolerated by those below you. It's *servant* leadership that people almost immediately respect and want to follow. The key is to be the example that your work force wants to be. Being that kind of thoughtful, intentional leader takes a lot more work, but when you're passionate about leading other people it doesn't feel like work. If you're just in it for the money or the title, most people aren't going to authentically believe in you and follow your vision.

If you're a really smart owner, you understand that your #1 responsibility is protecting your equity and investment in your business. Is the family member the best for the job? If no, then that person should not be put into that role, as the investment will decay under poor performance. Why would you expect your employees to respect you as the owner if you're promoting a family member or friend over someone who is more capable and deserving? Your employees may go AWOL in reaction to a situation like that, and the MPs won't bring them back.

So the Business Sergeant mentality that family-owned businesses need to instill into their leadership teams and corporate culture is this: YOU HAVE TO CARRY YOUR OWN WATER. If you can't and everyone knows it, step aside for the sake of the team, because it's really hard to ask everyone to sit at the table with someone who hasn't truly earned his or her seat. You're a C player with an A last name that doesn't compute, and everybody at the table knows it. You should 100% deserve to be there, period.

So if you're on a leadership team and you have ownership, *you should be able to be FIRED.* Your performance should be held to the same standard as anyone else's. If you're a weak link, you should be replaced. If everyone on the team knows those are the stakes, then your leadership team is going to come together a lot faster and with half the brain damage.

A close cousin of nepotism is favoritism, which is somebody who's a drinking, fishing, hunting, or golfing buddy with the boss, who has some sort of relationship outside the office that gives them extra access. We all know that most small businesses have some form of F.O.B or *FRIEND* or *FAMILY OF BOSS* issue going on, and these are what I like to call *CULTURE KILLERS!* When Uncle Randy can come and do whatever the hell he wants all day because he's related to the owner, but everyone else is expected to follow the rules, those are culture killers. These are the water cooler discussions that tear down your culture and move you backwards in business.

As an example, a couple of clients I presently work with are grooming adult children to take over in senior level positions within their companies in the next 5–10 years and they have really done it right. These kids started out working summers sweeping out the warehouse, working in the mail room, and when they do get the keys to the castle, they will know every part of the company, how each division runs and how it shouldn't run, etc. I believe family members working their way up within a company—and especially those who have ascended to leadership positions—should have to work to a higher standard to combat the natural perception of others working around them that they had it made. Everyone should know that they had to earn it the same way an outsider would, and that they did.

LESSON 12 ★ Strong Leaders Don't Feed Their Egos

A weak leader is threatened by people who may know more than he does. I've seen this countless times—someone comes in to apply for a senior sales position, and the sales manager doing the hire says to himself, "Wow, her management resume is better than *mine!*" He may shred that resume because it represents a threat. In contrast, a really strong leader says, "Our team would be far stronger because of this person's experience, and I could learn something from her as well." Strong leaders aren't threatened by having talented and competent people around them; they WANT to be surrounded by hungry, ambitious, and talented team members.

If you're a boss and have someone working for you who is threatened by internal competition, you need to fire that person immediately. In the long run, they will cost you money you can't get back.

While people protecting their own piece of the pie happens a lot in bigger corporations, this behavior is even more dangerous in smaller businesses where you don't have 500 or 1,000 or 10,000 people to hide behind. When you have only 40 or 50 employees, or perhaps even as few as 10, one person's negative behavior has a disproportionate impact on the entire company. It only takes one person's insecurities to throttle the spirit and growth of an entire organization.

If you're in an ownership or senior leadership position, take a close look at the leaders working on your left and right. Find out whether you've got *real* Business Sergeants working alongside you or typical egomaniacs just in it for themselves.

Great leaders are always developing their talent and/or replacing lackluster employees quickly with talented people who align with the vision and mission.

This is a big problem I see time and time again in my work with clients. During my full-day EOS® coaching sessions, I encounter people who talk negatively about other employees. I always stop them and say, "Hey, I just want to point something out. I've heard you refer to this person a few times, and *every* time you're describing someone who is not in line with where the company wants to go. I have to call you out on it. Why is that person still here? What's the deal?"

A lot of times they can't really explain that to me. They'll stammer and try to articulate why they haven't taken action. Eventually, at the end of our discussion, they'll say, "Okay, we're going to fix this."

LESSON 13 ★ A Strong Leader Supports Middle Managers

The next rule of being a strong leader is that you need awesome Corporals to be a great Sergeant. What I notice is that middle managers in a business—the Corporals, the first-line leaders, the people right over the line staff—have a huge range in quality, from really sharp and squared away, to lesser situations where quite often the executives above them are effectively doing the middle management jobs as well. When I talk to executives and really start digging down into what they do on a daily basis, I ultimately find out the problem is that he middle management person is not doing his or her work, and, most importantly, is not being called out on it. I end up calling out the leadership team for doing *too much* work, and my next question is always this: what is your plan for developing your middle managers?

I've also seen companies where the management/leadership team at the top is very good but their middle managers are not well trained, not well equipped, and not well motivated. When Sergeants are not very good, it's very difficult to have good Corporals. Similarly, in business, great senior management typically brings along great middle management, which leads to great execution. A company like this is avoiding weak links in the chain wherever possible.

There are a lot of advanced management training programs for senior leadership, but not as many for middle management. That area of the company's labor force tends to be pretty under-developed. The takeaway here is the importance of having a leadership development plan at your company for those leaders who have the most direct day-in and day-out contact with your company's sales department. Having strong frontline leaders is crucial to your company's importance.

Check your rank at the door, I like to tell my teams, because even Generals want to hear the truth. Far too often in business, the CEO and top executives are not really collaborative with their middle-management teams. They're only comfortable with the command and control structures they've put together, which doesn't lead to a lot of communication and feedback. The military uses senior enlisted advisors to command level officers, so that a different perspective can be heard from the ivory tower. These Command Sergeants Major (the highest enlisted non-commissioned officer rank in the Army) help their commanding commissioned officers understand issues through the enlisted soldier's perspective. Their job is to make sure the enlisted soldiers are healthy, ready to deploy, well cared for and trained to meet the demands of their commanding officers, and those appointed over them. A commander needs to understand their true capabilities with their troops, and how they are developing their future leaders. The civilian equivalent to this is having junior members of the company be on a culture committee or steering committee so their voices can be heard when discussing ideas. A great leader listens to all parts of their organization, not just the leadership team, as sometimes a "bubble" gets created, and your view is limited to a few strong personalities views, vs. the larger organizations.

If you want to have an elite culture, you have your standards set for minimum, average and exceeding, and then put the right "A Players" on the field to help push the team toward your shared vision. An important frontline in that push is promoting and supporting the best Corporals, because they're really the ones who will make it happen for you. Empowering your Corporals in the culture will have huge returns—they're the frontline leaders, they're the bridge between the Sergeant and the Privates in the military, and in the business world, your junior leaders are the bridge between your newest generation of hires and the Senior Team Leaders they're aspiring to become. In the military, you have to keep your corporals challenged, and in the business world it's no different. The more inspired and fired-up you get your junior leaders to be, the more you can create a combustible culture where everyone in your company is working in synergy toward the same shared vision up and down the line.

Middle management is where you want your "servant leader"—somebody who understands management's goals and the reasons behind them, but who at the same time is also sympathetic to the happiness of the workers on the "factory floor." Your team and subordinates need leadership, and if you don't provide it, no one else will. As an owner, it's imperative to understand that all the problems in your company are *your* problems, and no one else is going to fix them for you. If you don't know what's going on in the ranks, if you're comfortably insulated in your office from the problems percolating in your organization, those problems are eventually going blow up in your face in a very costly way.

It's key for leadership to understand that if the workers are happy, you're going to have a healthy organization. As a good Business Sergeant, you have to make sure your corporals have everything they need to be effective in their duties.

LESSON 14 ★ Strong Leaders Mold the Next Generation of Leaders

The leadership team you've deployed on the business battlefield today could be entirely different just six months from now. If you're thinking, "Hey, I've had this team for the last five years, I can expect little to no movement over the next five," that's a mistake. It's important to have great leaders and at the same time be developing new leaders. Put promising people on a leadership development track, invite them to certain upper-level meetings, and give them access to top level decision making. Let them know you've identified them for management in the future.

That way, you have someone ready to step into an essential position if one of your senior leaders leaves the company abruptly for personal reasons, pursues a better job offer, or is out medically for an extended period of time. It's super, super important to be grooming people to take your seat all the time.

And as an organization grows, new seats will be opening up to the new level of business that success can bring. You land a new client and need to expand your team to meet capacity. You can fully take advantage of that opportunity if you've trained your people for leadership along the way. When faced with a leadership opportunity, they'll be that much more comfortable behind the controls.

FOCUS ON THE CLIENT
Solving a Family Leadership Problem at Wheat Ridge Cyclery

Wheat Ridge Cyclery, a legendary bike shop in Colorado, was a family-run business with a heap of leadership problems.

The company started as a tiny 400-square-foot outfit in the 1970s. Now they occupy almost a whole city block in Wheat Ridge, Colorado, with a 30,000-square foot shop, a mecca for cyclists. People drive three or four hours or more past dozens of other bike shops to go to Wheat Ridge Cyclery because it's such unique and special experience.

There was no consistency in the leadership. Not only does every individual leader need to provide consistent leadership to their people, they also need to show a united front and be on the same page. If not, the company is not being run with clarity.

Here is what Vice President Ron Kiefel has to say:

My dad ran the company from 1973, then my brother-in-law Gil ran it for 14 years, and I've taken over since 2008. The problem was that the ownership group was forcing decisions onto the management group, and some of those decisions were off-base because the owners weren't in the day-to-day trenches of the business.

We've made some big changes. For example, we took our management group down from 10 to 6, including myself. We sketched out the idea of what a crystal clear organizational structure could look like and really helped us streamline leadership in the organization.

Since we started the EOS process™, 40% of our management team changed over a two-year period. That was a pretty significant personnel change and it was uncomfortable at first, but as we saw the fruits of those changes, we became more confident in our ability to assess people in their roles. We were quicker to make a decision and say, "You aren't the right person for this company." We've been getting the right people on our team and it's been real healthy for our company.

In terms of accountability, each employee has a number or a measure that they're accountable for. On our Accountability Chart™, we've defined the measures for each seat. We have a better sense that things are getting done and being followed; we can monitor our business better and we've become a healthier company. When people know what they're measured on and it's the right measure, they do really well and they're successful. We also created some pretty audacious goals.

We're getting better at understanding the relationship between the Board of Directors and the management team. The management team is in charge of day-to-day operations, which is measured through scorecards and other tools, and the Board of Directors has fiduciary responsibility. The Board doesn't need to decide what models we carry on the floor. Their obligation is financial oversight and the management team is responsible for meeting day-to-day goals.

We set some pretty big Rocks and we failed at them the first few times. We learned from our mistakes. When you don't accomplish some things, you learn what's going to work and what's not going to work.

I learned how far to give people rope and when to cut things off, to make sure that we were getting through the right things and not heading down too many rabbit trails. I learned how to call people out on their B.S. We're able to say to each other, "You know, there's something wrong with that" or "I don't like the way that's said." We're much more open and honest with each other, and as a result we're much closer. And that's because my leadership style has changed.

Having the right leaders and getting rid of the wrong leaders is super important. Wheat Ridge Cyclery is a really good example of how changing the dynamic of the leadership team can lead to transformational change. Today the company has an engaged and open culture, and is executing at a much better level than in the past.

WEEKLY LEADERSHIP COMMITMENT SELF-ASSESSMENT

— Yes/No Answers —

1. Am I a leader because I truly love helping develop others? . . . . . . **Y / N**

2. Do I listen more than I talk? . . . . **Y / N**

3. Do I give regular feedback to ALL my Employees (positive &negative) . . **Y / N**

4. Do I ask if there is anything holding my team back? . . . . **Y / N**

5. Am I delegating "Stretch" tasks to them? . . . . **Y / N**

6. Did I have a difficult conversation or did I punt? . . . . **Y / N**

7. Did I apologize or admit fault for any mistake last week? . . . . **Y / N**

8. Did I give each team member a crystal-clear plan for the week? . . . . . **Y / N**

9. Did I help discover/develop the next line of future leaders? . . . . . . **Y / N**

8 to 9 yesses = We should clone you, you are awesome!

6 to 7 yesses = We appreciate your active leadership, great job!

5 yesses = Good work; you are making this a better place!

4 or below = You need to be more intentional about
your leadership position.

THE BUSINESS SERGEANT'S LEADERSHIP DEPTH CHART

To use the Leadership Depth Chart:

Step One:
Write in all Employees who currently have leadership responsibility (even if only one person). Option: Include top performers who have identified as potential future leaders.

Step Two:
Fill in their leadership assessment score from 1 to 10, with 10 being the best.

Step Three:
After all leadership scores have been given, place the leadership score of the person they report to underneath their score.

Step Four:
Draw a "X" next to any leadership scores under an 8. (This is now an issue to capture and discuss the gap between where they are and where they need to be.)

Step Five:
Circle any "X" where the person leading them has a lower leader score then they do. (Capture this as an issue to be discussed, as your up-and-coming leader is being led by a weaker leader—A players won't stand for this! This is a huge bottleneck for growing exceptional future leaders.)

Step Six:
Discuss and determine if the leader with a lower score can be re-trained, put on a performance improvement plan, or if they need to be replaced immediately with another leader with an acceptable leadership score.

━━ EXAMPLE ━━

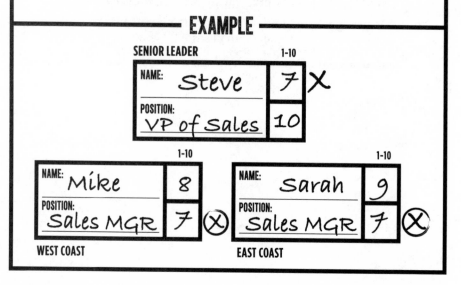

⚙ LEADERSHIP DEPTH CHART

1-10

NAME:	
POSITION:	

◀ Their score (1-10)

◀ Whoever leads them score (1-10)

SENIOR LEADER　　**1-10**

NAME:	
POSITION:	

1-10

NAME:	
POSITION:	

1-10

NAME:	
POSITION:	

1-10

NAME:	
POSITION:	

1-10

NAME:	
POSITION:	

1-10

NAME:	
POSITION:	

1-10

NAME:	
POSITION:	

1-10

NAME:	
POSITION:	

1-10

NAME:	
POSITION:	

 BUSINESS SERGEANT'S CREED

Modified version of U.S. Army NCO Creed

No one is more professional than I. I am a Business Sergeant, a leader of people. As a Business Sergeant I am proud of my team and will at all times conduct myself so as to bring credit upon them, regardless of the situation in which I find myself. I will not use my position to modify or skirt the agreed upon rules. I follow the same rules as everyone else.
I as a leader, I set the standard for others to follow.

Competence is my watchword. My two basic responsibilities will always be uppermost in my mind—accomplishment of my mission and the welfare of my employees. I will strive to remain technically and tactically proficient. I am aware of my role as a Business Sergeant. I will fulfill my responsibilities inherent in that role. All employees are entitled to outstanding leadership; I will provide that leadership. I know my employees and I will always place their needs above my own. I will communicate consistently with my employees and never leave them uninformed. I will be fair and impartial when recommending both rewards for above and beyond performance and accountability for poor results.

The other leaders of my unit will have maximum time to accomplish their duties; they will not have to accomplish mine. I will earn their respect and confidence as well as that of my employees. I will be loyal to those with whom I serve; seniors, peers, and subordinates alike. I will exercise initiative by taking appropriate action in the absence of orders. I will not compromise my integrity, nor my moral courage.

I will not forget, nor will I allow my comrades to forget that we are professionals, Business Sergeants, leaders!

CHAPTER THREE

One Team, One Vision

One of my favorite quotes that captures how important vision is to business success comes from Henry Ford, who said, "If I had asked people what they wanted, they would have said faster horses."

Ok, that's probably apocryphal, but it's true that Henry Ford didn't want to simply improve what people already had—rather, he had a vision that he was going to entirely transform transportation and that's exactly what he did. The first automobile was launched on the vision of a small business owner, and life changed for millions of people as a result.

Having a vision doesn't mean just asking people what they want. Instead, create a vision for what you think they need, and if you're right, you too can change the world.

Sadly, that kind of vision has been lost on much of today's workforce:

A whopping **88%** of employees Don't have passion for their work
according to a 2014 Deloitte study.[9]

(For those of you not great at math, that means only 12 out of 100 people who have provided you with products or services have ever cared about you. **OUCH!** To have a great business, we need to flip that number!)

A measly **32%** OF **Millenial** employees

were engaged in the workplace in 2015 according to Gallup.[10]

[9] https://dupress.deloitte.com/dup-us-en/topics/talent/worker-passion-employee-behavior.html
[10] http://www.gallup.com/businessjournal/195209/few-millennials-engaged-work.aspx

Deloitte Global Human Capital Trends' annual study found in 2016, after surveying 2,500 organizations in 90 counties around the world[11],

79% believe they have a significant **retention** & **engagement problem**

some 26% see the problem as urgent (They're deserting their units and clearly in search of better leadership and management. If you don't become a strong leader, you'll become a casualty of the same statistics.)

According to **Forbes,**

a partner in reporting the results of the latter study,

only 6% of organizations

believe their current process for managing performance is worth the time;

58% called their process "weak," with North American companies 20% worse than the rest of the world[12].

(If you don't have a process to manage performance, you're not managing performance.)

INC Magazine reported in 2015 that **actively disengaged employees** cost the

U.S. $450 billion to $550 billion per year [13]

In talking about engagement, I like to use this analogy: if someone's job is making donuts and serving coffee, and they were to look at it from the perspective that they're not just working in food and beverage service, they are really making people's mornings a little brighter and sweeter, they might start whistling while they work and have a little more pep in their step. I don't care what it is you do, there's a way to become inspired and engaged if you draw the line to the end-user's happiness. Unfortunately, very few people connect the dots all the way down.

When I'm working with a new team, one of the first things I ask them is: "What makes you get out of bed in the morning?" In their answers I'm looking for the passion, the goal behind the goal, the vision. When people just say, "Well, I make donuts," I tell them, "Well, the deeper response should be: 'We make the tastiest donuts in the land, and because of our amazing customer service our customers are happy beyond belief because of the extra care we take in making and serving them. We do it the right way because life is way too short for bad donuts."

[11] https://dupress.deloitte.com/dup-us-en/focus/human-capital-trends/2016.html

[12] https://www.forbes.com/sites/jacobmorgan/2016/03/03/deloittes-top-10-human-capital-trends-for-2016

[13] https://www.inc.com/ariana-ayu/the-enormous-cost-of-unhappy-employees.html

So as a business leader, it's important to come up with a little tagline that expresses your vision. It should be marketable but also short and easy for your employees to understand. No matter how you spin it, it should be something really simple to give people the choice to opt in or opt out.

I've coached Cascade Health Services, one of the largest American Red Cross training providers in the country. They must have 100 different courses in advanced CPR and other lifesaving procedures, and they're all taught by doctors, nurses, paramedics and EMTs. Their purpose or mission is quite simply, "Saving Lives." That really gets everybody excited because there's no greater gift you can give someone.

The difference between the military and the business world is that your people are not enlisting for six years; your employees can leave any time they want. If your vision is uninspiring and you're offering your employees piecemeal commodity work for compensation, how will they respond when somebody asks them "What do you do?" You won't want to hear the answer.

That is why 70% of Americans are disengaged in their jobs, a HUGE problem right now for businesses big and small. But it's the small business owner who has a better chance of changing that statistic. You can give people the option to opt in or opt out, but what you can't afford as a small business owner is people straddling the mediocre middle. Apathy, in my opinion, is an epidemic that crushes entrepreneurial dreams.

Your employees might be decent people not going out of their way to hurt you and your organization. But if they come to work just for a job and a paycheck, they'll do what's personally expedient for them when push comes to shove. That's a world of difference from employees who have pledged allegiance to your vision.

When everybody in the organization knows the vision and is in agreement around the vision, your team's a lot more likely to work intentionally toward a shared goal. If you have a focused and battle-hardened squad of business people who believe in your vision, you can literally conquer any hill (which is any market) and defeat any army (which is your competitor). Your employees *want* a strong leader to inspire them and take them to greater heights. Think about what you could do to create a compelling vision and be a strong and special leader others will be happy to follow.

LESSON 15 ★ Create a "Bigger Than Ourselves" Moment

As a small business owner/entrepreneur or team leader, creating an infectious vision is all about creating that "bigger-than-ourselves" moment. People really want to be part of something special, and being part of a winning team is just as sweet as individual success. Sometimes even more so, because being a member of a team and pulling off something huge by leveraging the talents of others is very exciting and rewarding. However, at the end of the day, if the vision is uninspiring, it's going to be very difficult to get anyone to follow you or gain any traction in your field.

Check the alignment of your employees' wants and desires, and how they match up with the big goals, not just the little ones. As Business Sergeants, we want to surround ourselves with people who are willing to commit to bigger goals, but they have to understand that they're going to have to make smaller 90-day commitments along the way to realize those grander ones.

The big point here is WE'VE GOT TO HAVE A BIG, BOLD, BADASS GOAL that motivates everyone on the team, that everyone can point to and say, "That's where we're going!" It's got to be big and bold and inspirational enough to get the team through situations where they're going to have to suck it up and tough it out. If you have a big goal that people can commit to, it's a lot easier for them to tackle all the subordinate goals that lead up to it.

Take LPR, a structural steel contractor I worked with. They're a $100 million company today. In ten years, they want to be a $350 million business. That might sound crazy but they have the plan and the people to get there.

Jim Collins coined the term BHAG (a Big Hairy Audacious Goal). You hear it used quite frequently and there's a good reason why. It's a big energizing goal that goes beyond the money. It ignites the passion, and gets people really whipped up and excited to be part of the journey.

Tersus Solutions, another company I coached, has perfected machines that can do massive amounts of commercial laundry with carbon dioxide instead of massive amounts of water. Considering the existing and looming water shortages globally, this company has the potential to truly be a billion dollar unicorn business because of what they do and the scale at which they do it. They have a great environmental vision that drives their company.

Once they're able to mass produce their machines, their numbers are going to go up like a rocket. Their footprint in the world goes way beyond saving people money. They're also going to save millions and millions of gallons of water that can be used for other purposes. A vision like that gets me excited. They're not just cleaning laundry; they're saving the darn planet while they do it. I think that's pretty cool.

To see another example of a great vision, let's take another look at Wheat Ridge Cyclery, which I discussed in the last chapter. The head of the business, Ron Kiefel, is an Olympic bronze medalist and two-time world champion cyclist, so when we start talking about a passionate team of employees it starts right at the top! They get to work every day in a store that feeds their passion with other people who share their passion (or as many of their employees say their "Cycling Habit").

When I started working with their leadership team to define their company's Core Focus™ (what they do and why they do it), one of the first points I said to them was this: "You guys know you're not selling bikes, right? You're selling memories. You're selling time with friends and family, bonding time. You're selling fitness, health, and well-being. You're selling a love of the outdoors, all those selfies on the top of the mountain, and all the happiness that goes along with it. That's what you guys do. When somebody rolls out a bike, you guys are handing out big grins and lasting memories. So you're not selling bikes—you're selling an exhilarating experience."

I was challenged by some of the team members, who hadn't bought into the "vision thing" yet: "What do you mean? We're just selling bikes."

I told them they were correct if they simply looked at bikes as a commodity, in terms of make and model. But if they looked deeper behind *why* people are involved in cycling and what they really get from it, they were involved in much more—putting smiles on people's faces, helping them stay healthy and physically active, enabling fathers and mothers and daughters and sons to spend time together in an active way. My big message was to have broader company vision.

"So let's not just sell bikes," I told them, "let's help people experience cycling in a remarkable and special way. Don't ever take for granted that you're selling so much more than just bikes—you're selling an experience. That's a special thing that enhances someone's life and that's bigger than all of us. So who's with the company on that journey, to enhance people's lives through cycling?"

LESSON 16 ★ You're Selling More Than a Product

Another example would be Zenman. Their passion is: "To shine a light on our clients, so they can tell their story." They're a digital marketing firm. Their whole job is to shine the spotlight, whether it's web traffic or thought leadership for their clients, so their clients are front and center, have everyone's attention, and are able to communicate their message. Enabling that game changing exchange for their clients is what gets their employees excited.

It's not what you're selling—it's the end result. A great vision means looking past the product or the service and really focusing in on the customer's experience. Instead of just selling them a product or a commodity, as your competitors do, sell them an experience. That experience has to become part of your sales and marketing messaging, how you speak to customers, what you talk to them about, your "why".

A lot of people, especially the millennial generation, say they don't really want to buy your *what* until they understand your *why*: "What are your business motives? There are ten of you that I can buy from. Why should I buy from you? Does your personal mission and values align with mine?" People like to do business with people who are like them. It's important to be able to articulate what makes you different from your competitors, so those people can find you and do business with you.

"Great vision means looking past the product or the service and really focusing in on the customer's experience"

LESSON 17 ★ Make Sure Your Vision is Shared

If we all have a shared vision that we're moving towards together, a healthy leadership team will be able to call each other out without anyone taking it personally. Everybody has an off day, and a healthy team means you can call people out on things that aren't right and then face them together as a team, helping each other improve in positive ways. I have a saying for this: "WE over ME is more important." Said another way, the name on the front of the jersey is much more important than the name on the back.

During my basic training, I was in a barracks with several dozen young men from every socio-economic status and geographic location in the U.S. I figured out pretty quickly that it didn't matter what culture or religion or neighborhood we came from; we were all in the Army together. The military put us into adverse situations with our backs against the wall. We had to rely indiscriminately on whoever was to the left or right of us. We had to put our personal beliefs aside to embrace those of the group. That's an extremely effective part of the military's strategy, and, admittedly, it's a little tougher to apply to a business backdrop. But in my experience it's essential in forging a team that works successfully together.

What we had in the military was a shared vision. If you have an inspiring vision and no one knows about it, then you really don't have a shared vision (which basically equals no vision). It's really that simple. So you need to communicate clearly to your employees: "This is what I believe in, this is what this company's about, this is who we're going to service, this is how we're going to do it, and this is what it's going to look like, smell like, feel like, and sound like."

Your employees should be as fired up about your passion and vision as you are. That's the level of commitment you need. Of course you want a lot of diversity of ideas and talent on your team, but this is an area where you need common ground.

Your vision is your company's fuel—it's what fires your momentum and your success. When people don't share your vision, their personal needs will outweigh the needs of the team every time. In a combat situation, that's deadly, but it can be nearly as dangerous in business battles. Lack of passion leads to lack of commitment, accountability, and ultimately, your business results, a cancer that will eat your company alive if you let it. If your doctor told you he found cancer in your body, he and you would naturally would take steps to address it immediately. Why wouldn't you on your team?

Everyone on your team should be marching together in the same direction, all in step with each other. It's not hard to keep a group together like that if that's how they're wired. The real effort is in the sorting process, finding the people who have that internal fire. One you have them, you can shape and mold them. They will bring a naturally reoccurring energy to the table.

LESSON 18 ★ Learn How to Engage Millennials

Millennials—Generation Y—will be the # 1 workforce by 2020, when, according to Forbes, they'll represent 50% of global workers. There's a lot of talk in business coaching circles about how to deal with Millennials, because most of the Baby Boomers and Generation Xers who run businesses haven't yet cracked the code on how to work with this group. Employers can't seem to get them to "lean in" via methods that have worked for previous generations. All the media tells us that they're lazy, they're entitled, and they ask "why?" dozens of times a day. Their mothers told them they could do anything that they wanted to, so they really think that's the case, regardless of the skills that might be required.

I think that's all crazy talk. The millennials I come in contact aren't like that. They're resourceful, they're hungry, they're super smart, they think critically in different ways than the Xers and the Boomers do, like, completely different. At Advision Marketing, all the junior leaders there are 25 or less.

To empower them, we have to define, very clearly and specifically, what their parameters are. They have to know what their authority is and what they're supposed to do and be given very clear direction. And once you've been very clear in where the boundaries are, you then have to give them almost total freedom inside those boundaries to operate so they don't feel micromanaged and demotivated.

The answer is simple and very old fashioned. You create a shared vision and give people special projects of strategic importance. You lean into that Millennial and say, "Listen, I need your skill set. I have a lot of confidence in you to figure this out. This is something I need done, and rather than giving it to someone with many more years on the job I'm going with you. Are you ready to step up and take this on for me? The whole company's watching and we're counting on you." As soon as you engage them on that level and give them some authority, they'll move mountains for you.

This has worked for several of my clients. The owners were able to engage the Millennials to share their vision and these businesses are now thriving! Millennials are far more capable than given credit for. They're very resourceful, creative, and solve problems in new ways. Their mastery of technology is in a different headspace.

Business.com, for instance, noted in 2016, "Millennials are continuous learners, collaborators, achievement-oriented, socially conscious, and highly educated. As a result, they are looking for more than a paycheck from their jobs… Adjusting corporate culture to appeal to this group is being adopted by more and more companies and for good reason–– it's a mutually beneficial relationship."[14]

But if you don't engage this generation, they'll surf for snowboards on the internet for half the workday and not think twice about it because in their minds, it's your fault. And they're right, because Generation Y knows how to get twice as much done in half the time with their knowledge of technology. But they have to be *engaged in the work* to do that.

I've seen frustrated Millennials sitting there thinking, "these old guys don't have a clue about what they have here and what I can do for them. If they keep treating me like a kid, I'm going keep acting like a kid."

What I've found is that if you engage them, if you get them to lean in by giving them more responsibility than you think they can manage, most of them find a way to rise to the occasion. It's really just something where you have to create the conditions for them to succeed. You've got to let them fail a little bit and you can't be too hard on them; instead, you really need to encourage them. Once you create an environment where they can take chances and figure things out on their own, they're going to perform in ways you never expected.

LESSON 19 ★ Without a Vision, Your Employees Will Go Rogue

As a business leader, you set the context for your team members and get people to buy into that context. If you don't, then you'll be herding cats instead of leading a team. When people are not stimulated and engaged emotionally and intellectually, they work just hard enough not to get fired (as Peter Gibbons so eloquently pointed out to the Bobs in *Office Space*).

If you do it right, your employees will be fired up with your vision. If you keep them tasked with full schedules, they're not going look for ways to entertain themselves at work. If you have an uninspiring vision, you're going to have to do a lot of management to get things done. A great leader knows his team's capabilities and deploys them on the business battlefield in the most advantageous way.

Could you imagine Tom Brady loafing onto the field and asking his team, "Hey guys, do you want to pass it or throw it?" His team would look at him like he was crazy: "You're supposed to have the plays, you're the QB!"

In business, it's the same translation: you need to drive people's energies, talents, intellects, passions, and interests by focusing them on the same shared vision. They can't be guessing at which play to execute. You can't assume they knew what to do, and they can't assume they know what you want them to do. As Steven Seagal says in the movie *Under Siege*, "Assumption is the mother of all F@$k-ups!"

When a company is run according to assumptions, you team will create their own vision, and then you've got a unit that's gone rogue, a situation that can be very difficult and unprofitable to unwind.

When you don't have a central vision, your department heads are going to step up and fill the leadership vacuum. They'll try to figure out what the vision is for their department, and the next thing you know you'll have five different fiefdoms in your company heading in five different directions. People are going to do what they're comfortable doing, and that won't serve the business very well. Instead of working on strategic, big-picture goals, they become much more limited and tactical: "Today, we need to produce 50 TPS reports." Your employees will be more like robots or machines than human beings.

LESSON 20 ★ Everyone Should be ALL-IN

Once the vision is established and communicated, people have the choice to opt in or not, and that's critical because you don't want people who are half in, but ALL-IN. Count on the fact that hidden within your ranks, on average, there's going to be that 20% who absolutely don't want it but don't make it known in clear terms.

It's hard enough getting your whole leadership team on the same page hard enough, but it's doable. Getting people to share your vision company-wide is a much more difficult task, and there's a couple of reasons for that.

1) They really didn't give a damn at their last job, and only kind of give a damn in this one (unless of course you're a part of the top 5% of businesses that have a business operating system and a great mindset to use it properly).

2) It's very hard getting them to understand the "why" behind the "why" if they're not fully engaged. So the ideal way to rope them in is to excite them with a grand vision like no one has ever excited or challenged them before.

They'll have that essential internal moment of realization when they suddenly say, "WOAH! I want to be part of that journey!"

If people set their sights, either in business or the military, on an end-goal that's not easy to achieve, if they want it as much as you do, a healthy level of competition and accountability ensues that just makes everyone work that much harder toward achieving your shared vision.

When adversity strikes, a committed team is all the more likely to pull together and stick with it. They are not easily deterred when difficult times arise. An employee who's just in it for the paycheck will be gone as soon as the going gets tough.

When we think small, those are the results we get. When you set the bar high and get your people fired up, then they'll act in a big manner and produce big results. If we set the bar too low, people who think big will be turned off by that small vision. There's no challenge for them; there's no path for them to climb their way to the next level and achieve the big things they're capable of achieving.

So if you have an expectation that's big, but haven't communicated that expectation or given the "why" behind your big vision, they'll be left wondering, "When do I get to live my dream?" That attitude will paralyze an organization. But if you're concocting a grand vision that's big enough to draw the big thinkers and validate their dreams of doing big things, you're going to have fired-up workers who will be giving their all. It's no longer a job, but a passion.

LESSON 21 ★ Use a "Simplified Strategic Planning Tool" to Clearly Establish Your Vision

It's an alignment tool that really helps crystallize your vision in a very simple format, versus a hundred-page business plan that no one's going to read or will have difficulty remembering. "Pick a big hairy audacious goal," to quote Jim Collins, and then have a marketing strategy to target your best customers. Where do you want to be three years from now as a company? Ten years from now? One you have that, develop a one-year plan and then execute a 90-day sprint to achieve those 1-year, 3-year, and 10-year targets. The entire leadership team is now on board with the exact same vision and they see a clear path to achieving the company's goals. Otherwise, as Yogi Berra said, "If you don't know where you're going, you'll end up someplace else."

The Vision/Traction Organizer™, a foundational tool developed by Gino Wickman for his Entrepreneurial Operating System® that aids your strategic planning, will help you find out what and if you're on target for your goals. One of the most important things I do as an EOS Implementer™ is helping craft a laser sharp V/TO™. When it's crystal clear, concise, and inspiring, we know we've done a great job together! Also, it's important to note that the plan has to be realistic, and if it scares you a little, then we are probably in the right spot, depending on what your growth goals are.

The V/TO™ makes you answer eight key questions:

The first is, what are your core values? Your core values are a simple set of timeless guiding principles, very clear behavioral guidelines for your employees. These are the "Handful of rules" for your employees to adhere to.

The second one is, what's your Core Focus™? This is otherwise commonly known as a mission statement. There are two parts to it. The first is your purpose, cause or passion, or your why. What's the goal behind your goal, that's bigger than money and bigger than ourselves? What inspires you? What is your reason for being here, whether you're waking up to give people smiles or save people's lives or whatever it is beyond the business result.

The next thing is your niche, your what, what exactly you do.

And then you set your Core Target™, your big goal that's the five to thirty years out. Then what's your marketing strategy to get there?

The rest of the V/TO™ is your strategic planning, simplified into 3-year, 1-year, and 90-day segments, along with documenting your long term (greater than 90-day) business issues.

To the degree that you can get everybody 100% on the same page with their answers to those questions, you will have a clear vision and direction for your company. And you communicate it quarterly, so everybody knows what's going on and how they're progressing towards the execution of the goals. What did we do last quarter? What are we going to do next quarter? Who's with me?

FOCUS ON THE CLIENT
Establishing a Vision at Advision

When I met Matt Walde, Founder and President of Advision Marketing, a full-service inbound marketing agency, they had a staff of five marketers, literally. They had no mission, no vision, no values, and no goals. Advision grew out of Matt's passion for digital marketing. He was able to grow the business to the point where he brought in a few more people, but they were so busy working that they never stopped for a second to think about *why* they were doing it. They liked the work so much and it was so interesting for them that they just thought they'd figure it out eventually. Many entrepreneurs and small business owners find themselves in this kind of situation. Matt eventually knew he needed help. Let's hear him tell what happened next:

We implemented structure and discipline, and developed a vision for the agency. From the ground up, we developed our five core values—no B.S., be fearless, give more value, love the puzzle, and camaraderie. We developed those in one afternoon.

From there, we rediscovered our passion for providing meaningful results for our clients. We refocused on our niche—maximizing small businesses digital marketing ROI. Then we developed our marketing strategy—our one-year plan, our three-year plan, and our ten-year target goals. In terms of vision, we were at ground zero when we started this process, and now I feel like we're probably 90% of the way to my ideal state.

One of the biggest challenges in establishing a vision is that it's hard to identify a purpose, a cause, or a passion in a for-profit company outside of growing the business and making more money. But the employees need more than that. Why are we doing this? I'm still really trying to focus and identify our why. We have a vision, we know where we want to be, we know what we're passionate about, we know what our purpose is. But we're still working on the why. That's a difficult task.

My process was to look at the agency as a whole and what we do. We're a generalist agency. We work with accountants, orthopedic surgeons, guys who put down garage flooring. If it makes sense, we'll work with just about anyone. We value all our clients, but the challenge is that it's sometimes hard to get passionate about the work.

I looked closely at my team. How do they behave? What do they like to do? What do they really care about? And I saw a group of people who really liked to travel internationally, who enjoyed getting out and seeing the world. And it's also my passion, something I've always wanted to do.

So I decided to start a new division specializing in travel, tourism, and hospitality. I knew that was something that everyone can get behind. We're working with more clients in that space, such as providers in France who conduct bicycle tours. I think the excitement and passion will grow as we do more of this kind of work.

And so that was my process in figuring out the why—to identify the passion in my employees and to adapt our work to match their passion. I think that will bring us closer to the why and we're very excited about this.

Some business owners might think that having a vision is one of those "softer" things in a company that doesn't really affect performance, but I can tell you that it absolutely does. For a long time I thought having a business in a cool industry was enough—a nice office, competitive pay, benefits, unlimited vacation, happy hours, Nintendos, etc. I thought that would be enough because that's the kind of place where I wanted to work. I just wanted to show up, do work that I enjoyed, and get paid for it.

But today that's not enough. You need to have a vision that your people can buy into with their hearts and souls. They have to feel like they're contributing to a cause when they walk in the door each morning. If the people who work for you don't understand why they're doing it, your performance won't reach its fullest potential.

Tool: EOS Vision/Traction Organizer™: Answering the 8 questions

Sticker Giant was recently named to *Forbes* Magazine's prestigious top 25 "small giants." These are "…companies that value greatness over growth. They aren't opposed to growth—just to growth at all costs."

Sticker Giant joined 24 other business recognized by Forbes with "…sound models, strong balance sheets and steady profits—all privately owned and closely held.

They contribute to their communities. They have been acknowledged as outstanding by others in their field. And they do things any business can learn from."

For more information on how to use the Vision/Traction Organizer™ and the rest of the EOS® tools, read *Traction Get a grip on your Business* by Gino Wickman, or go to www.eosworldwide.com to download the tools for free.

THE VISION/TRACTION ORGANIZER ™

StickerGiant

VISION

CORE VALUES	1. All In - Fully committed to SG. - Willing to do what it takes	2. Competent - Smart, capable and adaptive - Accountable to each other - Gain and Share knowledge	3. Positive Energy - Bring your best - No jerks, have fun

CORE FOCUS™	**Our Purpose:** We help people tell their story... Fast! **Our Niche:** We are the fastest at Product Labels & Promotional Stickers

10-YEAR TARGET™	Core Target- Faster! $50 million revenue by 12/31/2027

MARKETING STRATEGY	**Target Market/"The List":** People seeking to purchase a minimum of 250 labels and/or stickers in North America who desire Quality, Service and Speed. **Three Uniques:** 1. Speed - Fast 2. Easy 3. Guaranteed Top Quality **Proven Process:** Easy to use website with continual site optimization. Great Social Media presence with paid and organic SEO. **Guarantee:** Satisfaction Guaranteed. Let us know if it's not up to your standards and we'll make it right.

3-YEAR PICTURE™

Future Date: 12-31-2019
Revenue: $20 million
Profit: $7 million
Measurables:

What does it look like?
- 1 day production time for all products but silkscreen
- 24 hour service coverage, 7 days a week
- 10 core products
- Competitive large run pricing on site
- Sales & Account team
- 2nd Office in Longmont
- $250K in Gainshare bonus for year
- 60 full time employees
- Referral program 5% of sales ($1 million)
- International Orders 10% of sales ($2 million)
- Google SEO 1st page for Custom Stickers & Prod. Labels
- In house web developer
- Community involvement award in Longmont
- StickerGiant Branded Sponsored Event
- MIS is rock solid
- Sticker Tracker – status of orders in shop
- Wellness Center
- Full kitchen, including stove and oven
- New Purchase Order & Accounting System
- CFO hired on staff
- All Core Processes defined

THE VISION/TRACTION ORGANIZER™

VISION · DATA · PROCESS · TRACTION · ISSUES · PEOPLE · YOUR BUSINESS

StickerGiant

TRACTION

1-YEAR PLAN

Future Date: 12-31-2017
Revenue: $12.2 million
Profit: $4 million
Measurables:
Goals for the Year:

1. Reduce turn time on clear stickers & labels
2. Lauch Clear Labels
3. Sat / Sun shifts in Customer Service
4. 2nd Shift in production started
5. Silk screen pricing online
6. Reduce to 15 core products
7. Bar Coding for product status updates
8. Competitive large run pricing on site
9. New Referral Program launched
10. 3 Community Events sponsored
11. Full EOS roll-out
12. Fractional CFO in place
13. $100K in Gainshare bonus for year

ROCKS

Future Date: 07-13-2017
Revenue: $3.2 million
Profit: $900,000
Measurables:
Rocks for the Quarter:

1.	Hire an integrator	J F
2.	Reorganize Front Office Space (including conference room)	I M
3.	Reduce to 15 Products	J F
4.	Additional Shift Planning	R D
5.	White Gloss Label 1 day production time	R D
6.	Launch Clear Labels	R D
7.	Beta Test Bar Code	S K

ISSUES LIST

1. Technology backlog
2. New hires to fill holes in Acct. Chart
3. No in-house executive meeting space
4. Help Center / FAQ page on site
5. Software upgrades for work flow performance

PERSONAL VISION/COMPANY VISION ALIGNMENT CHECKLIST

My Personal Vision

I'm Motivated By (Goals) – Can I achieve those here?

Aligned with team?

	YES	NO
A.		
B.		
C.		

Brings Me Happiness – Will/Do I feel this here?

A.		
B.		
C.		

What Are My Superpowers? – Can I use them here?

A.		
B.		
C.		

My Top 3 Values – Does my team value what is important to me?

A.		
B.		
C.		

CHAPTER FOUR

Build a Great Culture: Be SLOW to Hire

Let's start this discussion off with the bottom line: building a great company culture is about hiring Mr. or Ms. Right vs. Mr. or Ms. *Right Now.* That's the difference between what culture really is versus what we *think* it is.

Considering the following stats that reflect on the state of culture in today's Corporate America:

According to *Forbes,*

88%

of Millennials prefer a
collaborative work
rather than a competitive one.[15]

According to *INC Magazine,*

"Nearly **85%** of Millennials
look at people and culture fit with prospective employers, followed by career potential."[17]

According to M.I.T.'s Dept. of Economics, "When we look at companies' web pages, we find that **85%** of S&P 500 companies **have a section dedicated** to what they call

'corporate culture,'

i.e., principles and values that should inform the behavior of all the firm's employees. The value we find most commonly is **innovation** (mentioned by 80% of them), followed by **integrity** and **respect** (70%). When we try to correlate the frequency and prominence of these values to measures of short and long term performance, however, we *fail* to find a significant correlation."[16]

[15] https://www.forbes.com/sites/robasghar/2014/01/13/what-millennials-want-in-the-workplace-and-why-you-should-start-giving-it-to-them
[16] http://economics.mit.edu/files/9721
[17] https://www.inc.com/peter-economy/19-interesting-hiring-statistics-you-should-know.html

According to the Harvard Business Review, "...**Engagement in work**—which is associated with feeling **valued, secure, supported,** and **respected**" becomes a *negative* association in,

high-stress, cut-throat culture."[18]

"New Deloitte research published in 2016 shows that culture, engagement, &

EMPLOYEE RETENTION

are now the top talent challenges facing business leaders. More than half of business leaders rate this issue **"urgent,"** up from only around 20% in the previous year."[19]

"A great company culture means **MORE COMPANY REVENUE.** Companies that have a great vibe and engaged employees vs. competitors with low engagement levels enjoy 2.5 times more revenue growth."[20]

LESSON 22 ★ Always Be Slow to Hire

Culture should be defined by the top and enforced by the bottom, both in a military or corporate unit. Most companies I've found take the opposite approach and enforce it from the top down, which almost never works. And the primary reason why it doesn't work, as I've found over and over again in my coaching, is that up top there's a high percentage of people (usually 20–30%) who are *not* in the right organization to begin with. Therefore, their concept of culture is inherently corrupted. They haven't bought into your grand vision and they aren't going to sell it nearly as hard as you would to the rest of your troops. That's not to say that most of the business leaders don't have great intentions in mind as part of their grander vision. Rather, it's the execution that fails because your culture is aspirational vs. inspirational. In that case, culture will never filter down throughout the company in a meaningful way.

Inspirational is inspiring people to do something attainable (big and scary is okay, but it has to be possible). Aspirational is trying to do something that you can't do now but maybe can do someday. When you say you're going to sell $100 million next year and you sold $5 million last year, that's a pretty big stretch and most people won't believe it. That lack of trust will permeate into everything else...so be careful that all goals are realistic and not a pipe dream. It's hard to be taken seriously if you're overly aspirational.

[18] https://hbr.org/2015/12/proof-that-positive-work-cultures-are-more-productive
[19] https://www.forbes.com/sites/joshbersin/2015/03/13/culture-why-its-the-hottest-topic-in-business-today
[20] https://www.linkedin.com/pulse/company-culture-when-vibe-dead-james-towers

The main point to remember is this: if everyone isn't buying in from the top down, the foundation of commitment to your vision among the troops in the field will begin rotting, which almost instantly devalues the caliber of culture you set out to create in the first place. Once that foundation starts crumbling, your engines of progress won't just start to stall but will eventually die on you completely. That's why it's so crucial for a business owner to be careful about the people he or she picks to be part of your culture. The people you hire have to want it as badly as you do, right from kick-off. As a Business Sergeant, it's important to remember that your unit isn't for everybody, and being slow to hire is the smart way to stop the wrong people from walking onto your playing field in the first place. To put it in a military context, define who you're going to be as a Leader and Unit by the quality of the troops you pick to represent you on the field of business battle.

Everyone in your company should not only be proud of your unit but ready to police it. That's community policing at work in its best definition. We all play different roles and hold different ranks within the corporate culture, but at the end of the day we're all fighting on the same side for the same cause—the greater good of the unit and company.

Culture is something that takes an immense amount of effort to create and sustain, and that effort starts with the proper selection of your staff. If you select the right people, you could be working in a garage and sitting on folding chairs and it wouldn't matter to your employees. The right people will want to be there. They will be passionate about the work you do, there's no "quitting time," and their loyalty isn't for sale. They're all there for the right reasons. In a healthy culture, it's not about the title before your name but the thrill of chasing a vision. Once you've created a vision, shared it with your people, and secured their commitment, you then have an intentional culture, not an accidental or makeshift one.

The next step is to be laser sharp about who you want on your team. Your core values—how we want our employees to be treated and how want them to treat us—is your high bar, your filtering mechanism, for selecting the people you want to surround yourselves with.

Someone who thinks like a Business Sergeant sets a high bar for hiring from the start and keeps it there. It's not an easy thing to do. If you don't set the bar high and just settle, like most of your competitors, you'll be able to fill up your team much faster and quickly attain a certain scale or size for your business. But if you rush 10 hires, I guarantee that you're going to be making another 10 hires pretty quickly, and with a great deal of unnecessary brain damage.

I've read studies where a bad hire, even a bad hire who's only around for less than a year, can cost 10 times the person's base salary over the time it takes to rectify the situation with the right hire and getting them up to speed of the rest of the organization.[21] This is due to lost productivity, the cost of conducting a new search, overtime costs in covering the people who are short, and all the extra training. And it's not just about the money. It's about employees losing confidence in the management team when they fail to select the right people. It's about the damage caused by the fact that it's much harder to un-hire somebody once you've hired them. If you don't set that bar high enough with a prospective employee, and he or she can't perform and has to be fired or "liberated" from your company, it's virtually impossible to make up the lost time, effort, and money that it cost you over the course of their brief employment.

I'm always preaching that if it takes you an extra month or two to hire each person you need, the pain you may feel by being understaffed during that time period is well worth it. If your current staff feels a little overworked while you're hunting for that right addition to the team, they can usually deal with it for a limited amount of time. What they *can't* deal with is you putting the wrong person in the wrong seat and having to pick up that person's slack along with the demands of their own jobs. That's what almost always ends up happening and chances are your staff will start resenting you for it in the long run.

But when you surround yourself with the right people, you can be yourself. You won't have to throttle back all the time, which is difficult, and taxing on the soul. Being slow to hire to create the perfect culture is worth the temporary headache of being short a person while you take your time to find that right replacement. The temporary pain of not hiring the wrong person is superior in every way to dealing with all the disruption of hiring the wrong person for your team.

When you do find that right person, he or she will fit in effortlessly because they want the same things you want. You absolutely have to train them and shape them, but make no mistake, when you're doing that with someone who's a natural fit: you just provide sunlight and water and they grow, almost on their own with only those essential nutrients. Don't do you—or your organization—an extreme disservice by trying to bring someone aboard who doesn't fit your culture.

[21] Careerbuilder.com, "More Than Half of Companies in the Top Ten World Economies Have Been Affected By a Bad Hire, According to CareerBuilder Survey," May 8, 2013

LESSON 23 ★ You Can't Motivate People From ZERO

You can't motivate people from one headspace to another. That might sound shocking or counterintuitive or just plain crazy, but I'm afraid it's true. We can create conditions that are motivational for people and it's really important that we do so. We can offer activities to keep the workplace fun and exciting and energetic. We can create conditions in the workplace that are motivational, but we can't truly motivate workers in a free and open marketplace.

One of the big differences between the military and the workplace is that in the former there's a lot of rah-rah stuff going on. You get up at 4:30 in the morning and you're doing physical training in the cold and rain, and yet everyone's sounding off like they just love being there.

We sing songs and chant in cadence as we march in the military because much of what we face every day really sucks, but we're all in it together so we to build unity in the face of adversity, and that alone give us common purpose and understand of each other's purpose.

In the civilian world, it's not like that. If someone walks into the office without having eaten breakfast, hasn't even had coffee, and has to go straight to meeting, that person has to motivate himself to do that. No one else is going to provide the motivation. There's usually not a lot of unit chanting and singing songs in the business world.

I like to joke that people have a pilot light, like a water heater or a furnace has one. You need that pilot light on at all times, so when you need heat it's ready to ignite your fuel.

The analogy works, because some people have tiny pilot lights that could blow out at any minute. It's fair to assume that someone who's 35, unemployed, and still lives at home in their parents basement has a low pilot light.

Then you've got brilliant and motivated people who are getting master's degrees by the time they're 25 years old. They're up at 4:30 a.m., they're working out all the time, and they're the people you love to hate because they have their stuff together so well.

Where does their motivation come from? From the inside. They're already motivated. Their pilot lights are always on and burning strong. Your job as the Business Sergeant is to recruit those kinds of people, to find out during the interview process what kind of flame they're working with.

The reason why this is so important is you can't really add too much to the fire someone already had. Bad management in the workplace can certainly extinguish or lower one's flame, but at the end of the day, good management really can't make it burn too much brighter, that's on them!

Internal vs. External Motivation

I've seen complacent corporate cultures where people are being paid bonuses just to do their basic jobs. In a couple of companies where I worked, they were essentially bribing people to do their jobs. It's no fun being a leader when you have to constantly motivate people with external rewards to keep your company running.

By contrast, *internally* motivated people who have a natural passion for the job are motivated by something that's much greater and more powerful than any external motivation you could give them. These people love their jobs so much they'd work for free if they didn't have to make a living. Their performance isn't going to be dependent on just their salary and bonuses; they're going to put extra effort into what they do because they have that internal passion and motivation driving them.

If someone really, truly wants something, and you can show them how their work is a direct line to achieving that personal goal for themselves, that's powerful. When that happens, you just need to get the hell out of their way and watch them do great things. If you can recruit and cultivate internally-motivated people, your job as leader is made about 70% easier.

LESSON 24 ★ Cool Isn't Necessarily Cool (Although It Can Be)

Imagine you're working at a tech start-up with a keg of beer in the company kitchen, a foosball table in the employee lounge, and a whole bunch of dogs lying at the foot of their owners' desks. You'd probably think, "Is this a cool company or what?"

But what if I told you this very "cool" company had a toxic culture, with people back-stabbing each other, not getting a lot of work done, and burning through cash even as investors have put their hard-earned money behind the company?

A lot of companies go out of their way to create really "cool" work environments. They put all their effort into the architecture instead of winning the hearts and minds of their people. I can walk into a business where I'm about to coach and within ten minutes, just by watching people, the way they interact and communicate, by getting a feel for the tone of the place, can tell if it's a healthy or unhealthy culture. A cool company might have creative work spaces and foosball tables, but at the same time be off-the-charts dysfunctional. There's no trust, no healthy conflict, no commitment, no accountability, and ultimately no substantial results. (Thanks to business team health guru Patrick Lencioni for that nugget in his book, *The Five Dysfunctions of a Team: A Leadership Fable*, Jossey-Bass, © 2002.)

Everyone is looking to be a part of something bigger than themselves that aligns with their personal goals and mission, and when they find that right unit to belong to, they feel like they're home, and it provides incredible comfort. Only then can the really good work come from people because they're not worrying about whether they're fitting in or have to check the online employment listings again. So be clear: culture is not just about having foosball and dog beds at the foot of your desks; it's about having a sense of home and *esprit de corps* within the unit.

One of my clients was Kevin Kelly, CEO and Founder of Altvia, a tech company based outside of Boulder, Colorado. The first day I walked into their office, I noticed they had 20 to 30 clipboards hanging in nice rows on what was probably an 18 x 12 foot wall. On each clipboard was a one-page questionnaire that was identical for all employees. There was a photograph of the employee in the upper left and the questionnaire listed each employee's favorite food, favorite movies, favorite hobbies, something about the person we might not know, a special skill they possess, etc.

I thought it was a cool display that was fun and helpful in getting to know the company's people. It told me that people were pretty high up on this company's list. They didn't have their products out front, they didn't have their list of their customers; instead they had their people up front, in a personal and caring way.

But there was a deeper connection. Any prospective employee would see what the atmosphere in the company was like. If she found people on those clipboards who enjoyed similar activities, had similar educations, similar beliefs and hobbies, that would warm her up for her interview. Or it might cool her off—perhaps she feels like a fish out of water among those clipboards. Either way, the company is doing a great job by letting people know very clearly: "This is who we are and this is how we roll." The clipboards were helping to attract the right people and discourage the wrong ones. I thought that was brilliant.

It made me say, "Alright, this is really cool, and really intentional! Let me look a little deeper into what's going on here."

I saw employees walking around the halls barefoot and there were plenty of dog beds next to desks. They had a really open and honest working environment that you could feel was real and authentic, not forced at all. Within five minutes I could feel that, and it wasn't just about the clipboards on the wall. It was about the *conversation* Kevin started by putting the clipboards on the wall.

This was a company that waited until they had the right employee, someone who was a match for their culture, and they took their time assimilating that new hire into their team. Because that new employee was aligned with their company's core values right off the bat, his or her clipboard fit neatly up on the company's wall.

By contrast, companies that aren't slow to hire can fall victim to what Vince Lombardi, longtime head coach of the Green Bay Packers, used to tell his teams: "If you aren't fired with enthusiasm, you will be fired with enthusiasm!"

In essence, Vince was saying, "Look, if you have to fake it, you won't make it. If you don't want that spot on the squad, make room for someone who does."

LESSON 25 ★ In a Great Culture, People Have Each Other's Backs

In the military, you have a reputation as a soldier. Whether you're a Private or a Lieutenant or a Colonel doesn't really matter, because what you do within your peer group is the same kind of stuff, just with different levels of seniority. My point is, each unit has its own culture based on the type of unit—Infantry vs. MP vs. Medics vs. Special Forces. The Military is very good at creating different castes within its own society, and they use awards, medals, ribbons, qualification badges, and insignia to show the different levels of sacrifice, commitment, and competency within each unit.

If you're in a company of 250 soldiers the elite 82nd Airborne division, it's literally the most fun unit to be in: everyone takes pride in exceeding Army standards, everyone's super-motivated and just loves to overachieve (that's why they wanted to be Airborne in the first place!). You can inspire your company's employees in the same way by creating a culture where everyone has each other's back and is putting in 100% because they love being on the same team and achieving great things together.

And if you articulate to your people exactly what's acceptable behavior at your company and what's not, they then have the ability to enforce those standards and are backed up when they do. When that atmosphere is created, your company loses that whole *"Us vs. Them"* mentality. Everyone feels they have a place and that they all belong to the same unit because a sense of community and involvement is alive and abundant within your company culture.

LESSON 26 ★ Recognize and Reward Accomplishment

I'm a big believer in creating healthy competitions in the office that also involve the employees' significant others. I might be your Sales Manager at the office, but you have a sales manager at home too. At a construction company I managed, I ran an end-of-the-year sales competition. I took my team out to dinner right around the holidays and announced the competition and its prize tier: First Prize was a Tiffany necklace and tennis bracelet combination, a $2,000 value; Second Prize was a set of diamond earrings, and Third Prize was a set of steak knives, right out of *Glengarry Glen Ross*. When I passed that Tiffany necklace around the table, it took a while to get it back because so many spouses wanted to hold onto it. When I asked who wanted to hear about the second place prizes, not a single hand went up!

Needless to say, over the next quarter, self-generated leads activity went up something like 500%, meaning that they weren't just running the leads that I was paying them to run. They had some open road and were knocking on doors, calling people on the phone, doing stuff that I normally couldn't get them to do, all because they had a shot at a Tiffany bracelet set for their significant other.

It's kind of funny how the numbers jumped off the scorecard during that period, and it was really interesting to see how many emails I got from spouses checking in to see how sales were going. I saw this huge increase in sales and it was because they had somebody at home encouraging them. The point is, when you get the families and spouses involved, when you get to know employees personally outside of the work environment, you'll get a lot of gains on the business side. We outsold that quarter by a long shot and that $3,000 investment in gifts was a drop in the bucket compared to the profit we put in the company bank account that quarter.

In the military, people feel elite, accomplished, and appreciated when they receive a medal, an award, a badge, a citation, or a higher rank. As Napoleon said, "No one will lay down their life for any amount of money, but they'll gladly do it for a little bit of yellow ribbon." In a business setting, we usually don't put people in uniform and give them medals, ribbons, and other decoration to display. But we *can* inspire outstanding performance through creative recognition as well as monetary acknowledgments. Doing so is crucial to keeping everyone on your team loyal, committed, and passionate, where they're pushing themselves to be the best players they can be for the team.

As a business owner, you have to create recognition and opportunities to reward high-level performance. I was running the sales team of a remodeling company where we set all-time sales records month after month. I borrowed a tradition from the sport of golf—the Green Jacket awarded to the winner of the Masters Tournament. I created a sales contest along with a green golf shirt with the company logo. The only employee allowed to wear that green shirt was the prior month's Salesperson of the Month. I also rewarded our top sales performer with preferential seating at our meetings, the best parking spot in the lot, and higher bonuses, and of course the best sales leads (highest potential dollars) we had to convert. I treated them like royalty, and after a couple of months of doing this, the production from my top five salespeople was up over 20%.

In another example in a restoration company where I was the V.P. of sales and marketing, I created an "A" team badge to wear on their company shirt, where we would hang a placard with the amount in dollars that they helped restore ($250K, $500K $1M, $2M etc.). Just getting on the "A" team was a big deal, a separate sales meeting with advanced training topics, the respect and admiration of new salespeople, and much more. Even customers got in on the promotion, as they would ask "What is that on your shirt?" then my representatives would be able to explain that they were the best of the best, and they had the experience to help them, vs. the many unskilled hacks in that space, giving the customer the confidence that they were choosing the very best rep and company for their project (WIN-WIN!).

That was 100% the result of bringing my military experience to the business world, and let me tell you, the culture I created on that A-team was the equivalent "uptick" of any top-performing military unit I served in.

LESSON 27 ★ Never Lower the Bar

Your employees should walk into your culture every with the conscious knowledge that it was very difficult to get in that door, and also very easy to be shown out of it. I've given you this cliché a few times already, and I'll probably say it a few more times just to be sure you heard it loud and clear, that if you're going to be in business, you have to be slow to hire and quick to fire. I find most businesses work the opposite way: they are pretty quick to hire and pretty slow to fire. When you take your time hiring somebody and nail it by finding the right person, it's a really sweet feeling. And when you make five or six really smart hires in a row, you've got yourself an A-team instead of a team made up of a few Bs, and a bunch of Cs. The A players can't really perform to their peak potential if they're not surrounded by other A players.

I like to point to a favorite saying of mine (and it's actually original to me): "High Bars = Great Cultures; Low Bars = Way Too Many Wrong People in the Wrong Seats," which can lead to CHAOS. Stick to your guns and say, "These are the types of people who really want this and think this way, and I'm going to keep the bar super high and not lower it at all!"

If you're going to be a Business Sergeant and lead people with military precision, you can't lower the standards. Those standards are set for a reason in the military—if they're not met, really bad things happen. Neither can we put unqualified people on the field of business battle. Yet we go into business battle with untrained troops all the time.

As the coach, mentor, Sergeant, and keeper of your culture, you have to remember that you only have a certain number of spots on your roster. Are they all the very best? An A player wants to play with other A players. An A player is excited by the high-level collaboration and competition she gets by being around other A players. Surrounding an A player with B or C players turns that A player into a B or C player after a while.

Forbes offers an important and relevant caution on those consequences: "When your culture goes south, your employees will quit… Every business problem is a culture problem. Whatever went wrong in your operations was caused by a breakdown in communication and a fraying of your cultural fabric."[22]

The concept of an A player can be different for every organization. You will define what "A" means in your own world, but understand the mathematics: an A player is always more profitable for you. An A player is someone who can literally do 2X output, 2X sales, 2X production, 2X utilization, 2X customer satisfaction. So whatever the results are, a real A player can do 2X what a C player does, so you should definitely pay your A players more.

If an A player is doing more, they should make more, and there's actually a market spread here that should incentivize companies to be more aggressive with their pay for A players. Look at the business equation I just gave you: if I have A player production at 2X and I pay them at 1.5X, I'm getting 100% more work while just paying 50% more money. There's an additional 50% of more profit there that the company essentially banks and can use to fund other A players. That's my version of a sustainable practice to attract and retain the best people.

So if you have five A players producing at that rate vs. a bunch of C players who are costing you more and producing at a much slower rate, what I'm recommending here is that you have a smaller, more capable team, and adopt a more military-oriented mindset in the way you run your company. If you do, you'll wind up with a far more profitable company. Once you decide as a team that you want to be an elite fighting force on the business battlefield, you'll be unrelenting in keeping the bar high, and you'll have commitment from your team to keep the unit in elite territory. But don't become complacent. Just because you have an elite unit today doesn't automatically guarantee you'll remain an elite unit next week or month. What's "elite" about an elite unit is that they understand that they cannot stay that way tomorrow if they don't do the training today.

Please don't lower your standards just so people can meet them. Keep your standards high and make sure you're recruiting people who can match or exceed them. I see companies lowering the bar a lot more and it always perplexes me. I fully realize that in certain labor markets you can't afford to be as choosey as you'd like. But accountability is key at all levels, and if the job is not getting done to the standard you've set, then it's time to set that person free to go find the right unit because they simply don't fit into yours.

You can't be emotional about this principle. Being quick to fire does not mean having an itchy trigger finger; it means that you're being decisive as a leader. If you were an NBA coach and a player on your team was consistently performing poorly on the court, you'd bench him regardless of his huge contract. In the competitive business world, your ability to be decisive could mean the life or death of your company. Any business owner or entrepreneur who's ever been through a bankruptcy, a turn-around situation, or just bad times will tell you that not holding people accountable contributed to that pain and suffering for everyone who was putting in 100%.

Lack of accountability is basically the root of all business evil in my eyes, so you can't afford to be emotional about this aspect of operating your business. Being quick to fire is like finding out you have cancer and going immediately to the doctor to treat it. Your employees will feel better about you as a leader because they see you looking out for the health and survival of the organization. Accountability is how we ultimately determine how committed we really are to each other and to our shared vision for the company.

LESSON 28 ★ Value Diversity, with the Exception of "Value Diversity"

It's important to remember that not every current employee or potential employee will be the right fit for your unit. And that's okay. In this country we've gone so out of our way to be inclusive to everyone that we've forgotten how being exclusive is necessary to running a successful business. If I'm a small business owner, my job isn't necessarily to be the most inclusive company.

To be really clear, I'm NOT referring to diversity in race, gender, sexual orientation, physical abilities, etc. We want and need that kind of diversity in corporate America. Understanding and appreciating that kind diversity is wonderful, but the one thing we can't be diverse on as a unit is our "why." The kind of diversity we DON'T want is VALUE diversity. Value diversity simply means hiring people who don't share your values in a deep way.

Throughout the multitude of industries that I've worked with, I've seen a common miscalculation where companies are WAY too inclusive when it comes to values. Build a wall around your business, and make it really, really hard to get through your gate. From what I've consistently seen over the years, companies that make it really, really hard to get hired usually have people climbing over the walls to work there. Set a high bar with your core values and scorecard and enforce those standards at all costs, because it will pay a lot more dividends in the long run than the money you'll lose by not doing so.

Use your vision and mission as the filters to make sure everyone stays on track. Your culture and company will be much healthier and more profitable in long run. Too much value diversity will cause unnecessary clashes and dramas in your company and culture. Most entrepreneurial businesses are less than a couple hundred employees; if everyone thinks about the business the way you do as their leader, then you're all rowing in the same direction to the same drum beat. The opposite culture is as messy as a soup sandwich, with people competing against each other and looking out for themselves instead of the team. Everyone has to be tuned into your company's core values, and too much value diversity can send your machine's gears grinding in all sorts of directions.

So if someone doesn't fit with your unit that's okay, because there's a unit out there that's a better fit for that person. The military benefits by having subject matter experts in all areas of their fighting force, and in business it's kind of the same thing: your company will be better served if that current or prospective employee finds the right unit. It's important that you, the business owner, set the right tone for your culture by being very picky about bringing in people with the right values.

I've already explained that culture is usually defined from the top down—the grand vision, this is who we are, this is why we do it, this is what we do, etc. Now let's bring that statement into the real world. Let's take one of the most commonly-heard stories in business: some horrible employee named "Gus" is allowed to stay way longer than he should. Finally Gus screws up to the point where the owner is forced to say, "Okay, I have to take care of this now." He or she reluctantly fires Gus, and for couple days employees will say, "I told you so" and "You should have done that a long time ago." But why weren't these employees saying something to the owner a long time ago? "Gus is really holding the team back! Boss, I don't think this is the right unit for him." That kind of conversation almost never happens, but it's much more important than talking to the boss after Gus is gone.

When we have value diversity in a company—when personal values are not aligned with company values—all kinds of problems can result. I often find that a company's best employees will become very frustrated working alongside with those who "don't get it." The last thing you want is tension and stress among the employees you rely on the most.

"After surveying over 20,000 workers around the world, analyzing 50 major companies, conducting scores of experiments, and scouring the landscape of academic research in a range of disciplines, we came to one conclusion: Why we work determines how well we work."

To help keep your core values clear for everyone, you must have clearly defined guidelines for how people are to behave in the workplace. Everyone must know how to fall in line with your core values as they do their day-to-day jobs. You can help people engaged by explaining the how behind the why—how does each employee put into practice the core value of the company?

Without alignment between roles and values, you always risk disengagement. According to a 2015 article in the *Harvard Business Review*: "After surveying over 20,000 workers around the world, analyzing 50 major companies, conducting scores of experiments, and scouring the landscape of academic research in a range of disciplines, we came to one conclusion: *Why we work determines how well we work.*"[23]

If you are "value diverse," your employees are likely to drift into what are referred to as "accidental cultures." If the senior leadership doesn't set the tone, rest assured that someone else will. Without a central vision to follow, fiefdoms and cliques will spring up, in effect hijacking your business. When that happens, all kinds of hell will start to break loose.

It's your job as a Business Sergeant to recognize and address that lack of commitment when it surfaces, by steering employees back to your vision, culture, and core values. Having clear guidelines for them to follow will get them back on the right path. A lack of defined core values or guiding principles, along with inconsistent messaging, will only lead to further confusion in your ranks. Great core values will always be a necessary filter to keep the wrong people out and let the right people in.

When your employees align with your core values, make sure you're constantly enforcing that standard. That's the central message of this whole chapter: define the bar, set the bar, and keep it there. Don't lower that standard for anyone: "This is the kind of business we want to be, this is how we want to act, these are the types of people we want to surround ourselves with, we're excited and energized by accomplishing the near-impossible, and we're going to keep our bar high." People who are driven in that manner will flourish. That is the secret sauce: setting the bar where you want it and never lowering it for anyone, ever.

Leading your company in this way may cause you and your team personal discomfort from time to time, but it's worth it. You'll never achieve your vision if you don't have that level of fanaticism among your employees towards your culture. That's what it takes to build a great company, and nothing short of that will get you there.

I meet a lot of people who want to have a great culture, high retention, low turnover, high engagement, and high profits. All of these are great goals and also wildly profitable on the balance sheet. That said, creating a strong culture is very hard because there will always be a hundred temptations to water it down. These temptations might make a lot of sense and seem expedient, but take my word for it, they're a trap! The pain and suffering required to get where you want to go are much preferred to the pain and suffering of failure.

LESSON 29 ★ Develop a Rigorous Interviewing and Selection Process

I can't emphasize enough how important it is to do the front-end work of being slow to hire. The bottom line here again is: TAKE YOUR TIME, do experiential interviews, and make it really hard to make the cut, especially when we're talking about hiring a key member of your leadership team. I don't think you can take too much time to make sure they're the right person for that seat at your boardroom table.

As a first step, I recommend using a personality assessment. Very few companies use them in the hiring process, and if they do it's usually at a pretty late stage, after they've already fallen in love with their candidate. Some studies say that people generally make a hiring decision one way or the other in the first five minutes of the interview. They then spend the rest of the interview being polite or learning more.

There are different assessments to test different things, but I think you should test candidates early so you can automatically disqualify those who aren't a good fit or don't even have a chance of getting into the basket. It saves a lot of time and money involved in needless processing and interviewing, and allows you to focus your energy on people who actually have a chance to fit in.

Once you have a core group of promising candidates, put them through a rigorous interviewing process that will enable you to separate the wheat from the chaff. Ask experiential questions. For example, ask the candidate to describe an initiative that failed at their previous company. Perhaps it was something no one wanted to pick it up and run with it, but your candidate grabbed it and got it done. Ask the candidate to describe in detail what he or she did, the actions they took to seize initiative and solve the problem.

If I'm hiring someone for a sales position, I'll ask that person how they found prospects in ways you wouldn't normally expect. Anyone can be handed leads all day long and close enough of them to keep their jobs. But if you ran out of leads and needed five more sales to meet your quota, how did you get them? How did they step out of the box or become creative in that situation? That's the kind of information you want to find out.

Ask experiential questions in the interview and let the candidates tangibly describe how they solved problems, achieved goals, and exceeded expectations. Create the framework of what you want them to do at your company and then probe them for examples of how they exhibited similar behavior in the past. Ask questions in a manner that doesn't tip them off to where you're going.

At the same time, you've got to do a hell of a lot more than just ask great interview questions. There will always be people who will interview well but turn to be flops after they're hired. On the flip side of that, some people are highly competent but don't interview well.

That's why I'm a big fan of trial employment. If you interview someone who's convincing, invite them to work at your company for a day or two or best case scenario a full trial week. You'll pay them for their time, whether or not they work out. This gives you a perfect opportunity to find out what they're like in action. Have them work for a full week if possible, because nobody can fake it for a whole week. At the end of the trial week either make them a solid offer or give them a check and say, "Thanks for trying. Good luck in your search."

I also like to take people out for dinner, bowling, shooting pool, golfing, or another kind of an activity. You can find out a lot about people in those situations. How do they conduct themselves? What do you pick up about them? Are they a good fit for your culture? You'll be able to find out important things that a standard interview can't tell you.

LESSON 30 ★ Work Can Also be Fun

Maintaining morale in your unit is a key kindling to keep the group's passion aflame and roaring, where your culture is a living and breathing presence that is owned by everyone. If you have good unit cohesion and culture, people will work together when facing adversity.

As a Business Sergeant building your culture, be unrelenting in finding the right people for the right seats, and create a culture that rests on high trust and high performance. At the same time, create a fun environment where your employees can work hard but also involve their families in quarterly company activities to forge closer ties and loyalty, as well as honor the sacrifice of the long hours for both significant others and employees alike.

It's important for your employees to see you take an interest in them, to truly get to know who they are. If you make your company feel like family, your employees will embrace your culture and become as committed as you are to the mission, with their families rooting them on all the way.

FOCUS ON THE CLIENT
Learning to Use Culture Tactically at Altvia

One of the companies I coached, Altvia, a provider of flexible, web-based software solutions in private equity, had a strong cultural foundation in place, but they didn't necessarily use it to hire and fire. They were able to define their culture pretty easily, but they didn't realize how powerful their culture could be until they fully utilized it.

My coaching goal was to provide Altvia with a framework to say, "Using our culture as a foundation, here are some of the more tactical things that have been missing." It was time for this company to really lean on culture and put it to work in a more operational way.

Let's hear from Kevin Kelly, Altvia's CEO and Founder:

Using culture tactically in an organization basically means that you're using specific methods and approaches to bring culture into the organization in a more conscious way. Another way of saying it is that we're now a culture that thinks about culture. Every company has a culture. But is it the culture that you want? Is it consistent? Are you doing things that create confusion? Are elements of the culture working against each other without your knowledge?

We shined a light on our culture, not only on what we want it to be, but in how it's being reinforced. The EOS® tools and Chris's inputs have helped us identify areas where we were reinforcing things that we didn't want in our culture. We were very receptive to this approach, given the struggles we had had getting traction with some of the other methods and tools we had tried.

Our company is about ten-and-a-half years old, and from day one, we were very, very focused on culture. But when we started a little over two years ago, we were able to document in a more direct way what our core values were and then develop a mechanism for actually implementing those core values throughout the company. Before this we were inconsistent in how we referred to our core values. Sometimes we'd have four core values and then we'd have six. We became really consistent in how we define our core values and in how we use them. We developed structures that made our culture accessible, more a part of everyday life in the company in a more natural way. We now have four core values and are very consistent about them.

We have a really simple framework for using our core values as a really simple tool that we use in our review process, a kind of scorecard for employees. And by having our values more consistently and succinctly defined, it also allowed us to incorporate them more into our hiring process. How does this person line up on this specific core value? It gave us a better, more objective framework for hiring and employee reviews. So that was a big thing.

One of the EOS tools that helped us tremendously is Vision/Traction Organizer™. It helped us to identify the core purpose and core values of the company. On everyone's desk is a laminated copy of our V/TO™, spelling out our core values and our core purpose.

We use our culture as a framework for deciding to let people go. We have also used it to shift people around, to identify behavior that's aligned with our core values versus lack of performance. The right person is someone who aligns with the core values. And the right person in the right seat is someone who understands what they're supposed to do, who has the capacity to do it, and who has an interest in doing it.

Our culture is so much more ingrained in everything we do. Using culture tactically has given us much more structure and foresight in hiring and firing decisions.

For example, we want a culture where there's good work-life balance, but we also have a culture where we want people to stay late and get things done when they have to. You have to recognize that sometimes those two values are in conflict, depending on what you reward or what you notice. If I send an email thanking an employee for working all weekend, that's inconsistent with a culture of work-life balance. And it's not so much that you choose one extreme or the other. Instead, I can find a middle ground between the two. But just understanding that there are confusing or conflicting messages helps you proceed accordingly.

One of our core values is transparency in the operations of the company. Our quarterly state-of-the-company meetings used to last between two and five hours. They would kind of ramble on and people would lose interest. We now have a much tighter reporting cycle and a much better framework for conducting our meetings. We can be transparent, we can get people the information that they need, and we can do it in an hour. We've improved our reporting abilities and the metrics and key indicators that we're tracking. Our people have easier access to that information, whether it's reports or dashboards or things like that.

I think we're incredibly well positioned for 2017 to be a breakout year as a result of the work that we started two years ago with him.

One of Chris's mantras is "slow-to-hire and quick-to-fire." It's so fundamentally true, and yet at the same time really hard to come to terms. But when you have simple metrics or a simple framework for measuring performance, when you look at hiring and firing through that lens, it makes it a lot easier to make the right decisions. Using culture tactically has allowed us to be more proactive with employees. We've been able to have very, very candid conversations with individuals that enabled us to avoid firing them. We were able to really zero in on what the problem was and correct the behavior. In the past we would've been more inclined to say, "Gosh, this guy's really not performing in that role. I guess we're going to have to let him go." Or he would decide to opt out on his own. Now we're more able to help employees improve their performance or move to a different position if need be.

CORE VALUE EXAMPLES

Here are a half dozen core value sets from my clients, as I read each one they remind me of that particular team. Notice the re-occurring thread of commitment to the organization in each of these?

Zenman

Recently Voted #1 Digital Marketing Company in Denver by Colorado Business Magazine)No bullet points as CEO Keith Roberts wanted no explanation—"less is more."

Core values:

1. Industry Innovators
2. Process Gurus
3. Quantitative Creativity
4. Perpetual Karma
5. Reputation Guardians

Bonanno Concepts

8 unique highly rated fine dining establishments in Denver, CO.

Core values:

1. Pride
- We are Positive & Enthusiastic — Get Stuff Done!
- No Problems, only solutions
- We are Owners, not renters

2. Excellence
- We are Committed, Competent, and Consistent
- We learn, we lead, we grow

3. Family
- Together we are better, always respectful and accountable
- We are pro-active and collaborative
- We serve our community

Cadence Capital Investments

Build to suit and commercial real estate development.

Core values:

1. Respect the real Estate Ecosystem
- We serve the well-being of all stakeholders
- We think long term

2. Energy
- We are persistent and adaptive
- Activity creates opportunity

3. Intellectually Agile
- Quick on our feet
- Curious and street smart
- Creative

4. Action Orientated
- 100% Effort
- Bold but disciplined

5. Calm in the face of the storm

⊗ CORE VALUE EXAMPLES

Famous Dave's of America

Award-winning BBQ restaurants with over 100 locations nationwide

Core values:

1. Be famous
- By practicing "Good, Better, Best, Never Let It Rest"
- By treating others better than they expected to be treated
- In your daily actions and interaction

2. Be real
- Treat everyone with respect and acceptance
- By being your "Famous" Self
- Always being open and honest

3. Kick butt and have fun
- By delivering Famous results
- By demonstrating passion for our BBQ culture
- Through teamwork and your Famous attitude

Bridgeview IT

National Technology Recruiting Firm

Core values:

1. Driven
- We are Persistent and Resilient
- We are committed Partners

2. Positive
- We appreciate and respect our Candidates, Clients, and Employees
- We are authentic and optimistic

3. Focused
- We have a deep knowledge of our clients' and candidates' needs
- We are 100% committed to the right fit

Milo Construction

Commercial construction firm in Boulder, CO

Core values:

1. Courage
- To be ourselves and stand up for what is right
- We seek resolution through healthy and constructive conflict

2. Own It
- We own our results, we take initiative, and follow through all the way
- We give no excuses and we are accountable to each other

3. All-In
- We are committed to elevating the construction experience for our clients and employees
- We are fiercely committed to supporting each other while we have fun along the way

⊕ SLOW TO HIRE CHECKLIST

All of the main checkpoints to ensure a great hire (1/3 initial office interview/experiential interview, 1/3 assessments, and 1/3 resume and references) and a scoring matrix to rate the "whole body" of their previous experience and potential fit

1. Does this candidate have ALL the minimum experience requirements that you set before meeting them?

2. Did all that participated in the interview process feel they a rock-solid culture fit for your team?

3. Is the compensation offered in-line with what the candidate was earning before?

4. Is there a legitimate reason that this strong candidate is available, and do they have proof of top 20% performance at their last company?

5. Would you be concerned if your current team had to compete against this candidate in the open market if they worked for your biggest competitor?

6. Did everyone in your company's multi-step interview process (Traditional and experiential) feel that this candidate would be a great asset to your organization (skills wise?)

7. Are they better equipped to perform than the last person that held that position?

8. Have they taken various assessments to determine if they have what it takes to do the job?

9. Have you spoken to several provided references and have you asked for additional references to those that they have lead and managed before if in a leadership role?

10. Have you done a criminal background check (Asking for all counties that they have lived in)

11. Have you done an online search for prior and recent behavior that would reflect poorly on your company? Are any of their views expressed differently than what you were told?

12. Have you taken the candidate out in a social setting and observed how they interact with others?

CHAPTER FIVE

Accountability: Quick to Fire

"Standards are not rules issued by the boss; they are a collective identity. Remember, standards are the things that you do all the time and the things for which you hold one another accountable."

—Mike "Coach K" Krzyzewski, Duke Basketball

"My job is not to be easy on people. My job is to take these great people we have and to push them and to make them even better."

—Steve Jobs

As Monster.com, the largest online employment placement hub in the United States work force, correctly quips, "Unless your last name is Trump, firing an employee is probably one of the least enjoyable parts of owning a business. And for a small business—where boss and employees often think of themselves as a 'family'—terminating an employee can be especially tough."

Once you get everyone to see the negative results of a lack of accountability, once you paint a vivid picture of the pain it causes and show how easily it can be avoided with some common goals and a little community policing, everyone should come on board. They will help you root out the weak links through the strength of their shared commitment to keeping the bar consistently high.

In an entrepreneurial business, you're not working for the government or a huge multi-billion dollar corporation where accountability can be very low and getting fired takes some real doing (Example: you're regularly only putting in 25% effort and spending lots of personal time on the internet, joking at the water cooler, or finding a good napping spot). Most small businesses have a more direct approach: if you do well, you make more money; if you don't, the work doesn't get done and everyone knows it, as clients and profits are lost and you'll have to go work for somebody else and steal from them. That has to be the mentality, because none of these businesses I work with, even the larger ones that generate half a billion dollars a year, are immune from failure. Not a single one of them are too big or established to fail.

Again, it's as true in the military as it is in business: you're only as strong as your weakest link. That's the link that will fail first when you put some stress on the chain. So, take a very strong look at your chain *today* and on a regular continuing basis (I recommend quarterly). When taking that look, here are some lessons on how to change your so-so culture to one that is more militaristic, entrepreneurial and oriented around commitment from everyone at the table.

LESSON 31 ★ You Must Have an Accountability System

An operating system provides a safe space for leaders to understand who needs to go and who needs to stay. In my experience, it's very difficult to explain the ecosystem that needs to be created in order for true accountability to exist, and that's the essence of what this chapter is about. But when you have a business operating system in place for accountability, that gives you visibility into who is or is not doing what and how well they are doing it. When you have systems in place that are followed by everyone in the company, it's much easier to identify a weak link in the chain. Secondly, and just as important, what does poor performance have as a *consequence*. There must be consequences if you hope to have any sort of discipline and accountability, and it shouldn't start the day you fire someone. It should start early on and it must be equally applied all the way up and down the chain of command.

I've yet to see a business that can't be helped by installing a business operating system, where you have the visibility to make these calls about prioritizing and accountability. With every client where I've helped them implement a system, I've heard them say, "Wow, I can't believe the clarity and communication and the accountability that's happening at my company by just doing a few simple things that you taught us. It is a night and day difference."

Once you've got that system in place and your employees understand how it works, then you're either meeting the standard or you're not. Without that steel trap of accountability, a lot of times people can justify why they didn't do something. They're able to rationalize why their priorities aren't aligned with the company's priorities. With an accountability system, you nip that in the bud. You need three things to create fire: heat, fuel and oxygen, take any of those three away, no fire. Think about what the ingredients are for your business to succeed (burn) or fail (extinguish)? Add or remove them for a similar effect; accountability is one of the main ingredients for success in business.

LESSON 32 ★ Be Quick to Fire

You can't always be Mr. Nice Guy or Ms. Nice Lady because the very survival of your culture is at stake. I see it all the time with the leadership teams I work with—they're afraid to fire someone when they need to. The fear of having a difficult conversation can neuter otherwise great leaders

I'll give you a vivid example of another turn-around situation I was brought into: I'll never forget walking into this previously very successful construction company's leadership team meeting. They had lost their way and were on the verge of going out of business because they had a huge staff of friends and family, not enough sales, a make believe sales pipeline, and still no one wanted to fire anybody because they all felt like it just was just going to turn around because they were about to enter the busy season. I got right down to it and asked the room, "What's worse? You lay off ten people today or all fifty of you are gone in a month or two?"

Nobody wanted to answer me. So I persisted, "You have to do what's right for the majority. I can understand this is uncomfortable, but if you fail to make this decision, everybody's going to lose their jobs and this leadership team's going to be the cause. Can you explain that to the children of those families? Your employees need you to make some tough decisions very quickly now in order for the company to survive. The decision will have to be made one way or the other."

Take *Fortune* magazine's word for it: "Management is responsible for telling individuals if their performances were not up to snuff, putting them on a program to fix it, and then removing them if corrections couldn't be made. If management was unwilling to do that simple job, they weren't managing."[24]

I see that unwillingness all the time, and my reaction is almost always the same: "Really? You're going to lose your business because you're afraid to let someone go?"

So many people in business think this a negative to do, but it's NOT. If someone is not in the right unit, we need to send that person somewhere where he/she will be happier. It's vitally important to not keep someone around in a role where they're consistently failing.

Naturally, it goes without saying that firing an employee should be a last resort, but when it becomes obvious that employee doesn't belong (and, most times, the employee doesn't feel comfortable either), then it's the unhealthiest possible path for both parties to maintain the status quo. These people are miserable at your company, and everyone else on the team is miserable having to work with that unhappiness and corresponding poor performance. So if we're going to be slow to hire and keep the bar really high, then we have to be quick to cut ineffective employees from the squad.

Maintaining high levels of organizational health, teamwork, and leadership is hard to do because not everybody is 100% on their game all the time. So I'm *not* talking about summarily firing employees for making small mistakes. I'm talking about having an agreed-upon system and scorecard that makes it clear when you need to have that tough conversation, even if it's uncomfortable for both of you. Let me assure you, it will be MUCH easier for you to have that difficult conversation as soon as they get off track rather than waiting for the point where you have to fire them.

Forbes magazine, an authority in studies on the subject, wrote, "making any mistake once was OK, but repeating that same mistake a second time was NOT OK. The hard, fast rule was that if you made any mistake for the first time, the entire team would have your back in fixing that mistake if anything went wrong. However, if you ever repeated the mistake a second time, then you were 100 percent on your own to face the consequences."[25]

[24] http://fortune.com/2013/03/05/why-layoffs-are-for-lazy-corporate-overseers

[25] https://www.forbes.com/sites/amyanderson/2013/04/17/good-employees-make-mistakes-great-leaders-allow-them-to

LESSON 33 ★ A Strong Leader Has Difficult Conversations

Being an effective Business Sergeant often means being brutally honest with people. Too often in the corporate world, people are used to receiving a piece of bad news sandwiched between two compliments. This makes for a very passive-aggressive environment where you're no longer speaking the truth when it needs to be told.

The strong leader will say, "Listen, a lot of people are depending on John's leadership. The position needs someone new because John can't lead in the way we want and need. I'm sorry if this is uncomfortable for everyone to hear, but it's not working and we're going to make a change." That's real leadership. Unfortunately, it usually takes people months, if not years, to get to the point where they can have those difficult conversations.

A strong leader is not overly emotional about winnowing out poor performers. They remove the emotion from the decision by staying focused on the greater good: "What do we need to do to accomplish this mission?"

Here's where having a military mindset will help: if you're a member of a military unit going into a hostile area, you need to have a lot of confidence in the person to your left, right, front, and rear. When you don't have that confidence, you're not fully focused on the mission in front of you. You're constantly looking over your shoulder to make sure someone isn't slacking off and with that mindset really bad things can happen.

Again, the correlation between business and war is obviously not an exact one. In business, the stakes are not nearly as high. You may not lose your life, but you still might go bankrupt. That's why leaders need to make tough and uncomfortable decisions to bring about the change necessary for the organization to move forward. It means doing the sometimes unpleasant or unpopular things when someone on your team is not giving 100%. If you're a leader, and you can't handle that responsibility, I'll make it easy for you... YOU are not giving 100% and you should seriously re-evaluate if you should be in a leadership position.

LESSON 34 ★ You Can't Make Everyone Happy

In one of the mortgage companies I coached, a senior loan processor was making six figures a year but doing maybe $30,000 worth of work. She had a ton of personal problems, had gotten really political, and easily became emotional under pressure. She was a distraction holding back everyone else and the owner was having trouble letting her go. Her twenty chances to change had come and gone.

On paper, discharging this person was an easy decision, but it was challenging for me to get the Leadership team to see that this person's problem in turn caused problems with everyone else's execution. It was a contentious situation, but she finally agreed to move on. The company put together a transition plan to find a replacement; they gave her a nice parachute and discharged her from the organization. It was right thing for the team and the right thing for her, because her lack of commitment was costing the company tens of thousands of dollars, while everyone was walking around on eggshells every day, which is never fun.

If you have to tell somebody something ten times before they do it, that's not *their* problem—that's your problem. That's the worst kind of leadership you can have, because if you have to repeat yourself that many times you're probably not conveying the correct message.

I find that business owners, especially visionary entrepreneurs, have generous hearts, perhaps too generous. They can be soft when they need to be tough. That's how we get a bunch of half-committed people in key positions on leadership teams, or what I like to call "Senior Management Spongers."

Pissing off a few people can make a lot of people happy, and that's a good thing in corporate America! On *Star Trek,* Mr. Spock once said to James Kirk, "Captain, the needs of the many outweigh the needs of the few or the one."

That really sums up the essence of leadership. It's almost impossible to make everyone happy in business. So the way I look at is, "Okay, who are you going to piss off and why are they going to be pissed?" I think this is a really great question to ask and it's the approach I take with people I coach. I'll ask, "Are they going to be pissed for selfish reasons? If so, then let them be pissed!" Because if you're pissing people off for the right reasons, you're doing great work, and leaders in business could use a little bit more of that military mindset.

Consensus management will put you out of business fast. Yes, consensus is needed for many decisions, but it can also be a disservice to the mission, the company, and the employees. Better to rip off the Band-Aid and say, "listen, this is what's best for the organization as a whole, and it may be uncomfortable for a few people. If it is, let's see what we can do to make that transition easier for them, because ultimately if they're here for the right reasons, they'll understand." Even though some people might experience some personal discomfort, if it's the right thing for the company they'll get behind it.

So whenever people get pissed off, I want to know right away, "why are they pissed?" And anytime I hear selfish stuff, I call it out right away. I'll say it right to their faces in front of the whole room.

Everyone knows that average is the enemy of great in essentially anything you do. If you get used to being average, that's what your people will become and that's how your organization will be perceived. Once that average anchor gets planted, it can cause major problems when you try to raise the stakes for your company and employees down the line. Trust me, I've seen this too many times when I've helped companies turn their ship around.

LESSON 35 ★ In a Great Culture, Peers Hold Peers Accountable

A great example of accountability in the military is what we call "foxhole trust." I'm not going to fall asleep during my watch, because I want you to be safe and get some rest, and I expect you to watch my back when I'm asleep.

You want your people to have this kind of accountability mentality: "I would hate to let the team down because I would be very disappointed in myself." You want people on your team to be that committed, who want it so badly that they'll do almost anything not to let the team down. It's not acceptable for people to show up to a meeting smiling and appearing unconcerned when their numbers are way off. In the military that doesn't fly at all, but in the business world it flies all too well—and right out of the room with your wasted money.

As you and your troops rev up to start the march down the path to greatness, unifying your team around a centrally shared vision is central to victory. It's a concept I like to pitch as *"One Team, One Mission,"* because if everyone's priorities and levels of commitment aren't on the same page and heading in the same direction, things are going to become confusing and crash fast before you even take off. This is a stage of the game where you want to rely on your team to police their culture, where the team will correct their peers with a conversation before going to management. As you instill that kind of discipline into your team's shared vision, the road to victory will become that much easier to follow. There is no passivity in passion. When you see a communal confidence running through the DNA of your corporate culture, you will consistently produce great and long-lasting results for the welfare of both your company and employees.

Once you create a Business Sergeant squad that's really tight, your employees will police the organization out of their passion and commitment. When your employees know they have the authority to call out poor performance or poor behavior, you will generally see less of both.

This is a very effective tool in the military and it equally applies to business— people can't be committed only when it's convenient for them. They're either committed or they're not, there's no allowable in-between, and it's okay if they don't want to commit. You just need to let them know there's no place for them on the bus.

We only have so many seats at the table, especially on a Leadership Team, and as a business owner you have to take the attitude with your employees that there are plenty of qualified, hungry, passionate professionals waiting to take their place if they aren't committed to the mission and vision of the company. I like to tell my clients "Just think about that great employee stuck at another company that would absolutely crush it here, they are under-appreciated, sick of the lack of accountability and poor performance of that team, if you leave the bad ones here, you won't make room for them, and that is really sad ending for everybody, right?"

This doesn't mean you treat people like they're easily replaceable. Most employees are in fact much harder to replace than we may think, but at the same time don't be afraid to seek the very best talent available, even when you think your team is good enough.

This underscores once again the importance of your employees policing their own culture for consistent excellence. It's the very reason the military is such an effective operating machine up and down the line. In the very best military units, peers hold each other accountable regardless of rank. Soldiers can even be "peered out" in elite units like the Special Forces. It's unthinkable for someone without the right attitude or aptitude to be in one of those units. Elite units have a Peer Review process that weeds out those soldiers who don't have the trust and confidence of their fellow team members or instructors. You can endure an entire course and a day before graduation in the toughest schools the military have to offer and still be "peered out." Devastating news for the one soldier, but the right news for the many who have the right stuff for that unit.

It's the same in business. Every member of a team has to be accountable to one another because then they're being accountable to the company as a whole. If this is something done at the highest professional levels of the military, why not have some sort of peer review process in an entrepreneurial/corporate setting? If that process indicates a problem with an employee, it enables you to actively deal with that problem.

And it has to be the same among your Leadership Team members: everyone's heard the famed "Code Red" term from the Tom Cruise/Jack Nicholson movie *A Few Good Men*, right? Sometimes it's necessary for your employees to perform an Office Code Red, where they take aside that employee or team member who's slipping and set them straight before word ever gets up the chain to the boss (no soap bars in socks, just a conversation!) It's called looking out for your fellow troops, having their back by giving them a kick in the butt if necessary for not being a team player. If they really want to be on the team they'll thank you for it. They may not have even been aware that they were slipping up.

You should have the expectation that your employees all want to keep the bar raised as high as possible. You're the last person they want to hear from about poor performance, so you should encourage a culture where your people feel comfortable having an open and honest dialogue about difficult topics before they ever even have to reach your ear.

Now, for the benefit of your employees, what is an "Office Code Red?" They should think of it as an intervention at the employee level, where people of equal rank can take each other aside and say, "Listen, we're not meeting our productivity goals because you keep screwing up…" Peers identify disruptive behaviors and are able to tell that person, "this isn't going to work. You either need to figure this out and become one with the program, or we want you to think about moving on. We think something rapidly needs to change. Please follow our rules!"

In business there's no room for the intensity of *Full Metal Jacket*, with drill sergeants screaming in a soldier's face, but there is room for exchanging open and honest words. You could even call it Corporate Tough Love. It has to be handled carefully, not emotionally or in a hostile way, but encouraging a culture of self-policing among your staff will prevent problems from getting worse or even stop them before they become habits.

If your employees care about the team, they'll be self-motivated to monitor their peers. They will know there is something of value to lose and they will want to protect it.

Again, to help everybody stay accountable, you need to use a scorecard. Without one, you're just going by your gut, rather than using hard data that cannot be refuted.

Highly accountable teams run circles around those that just talk about executing. If I tell you I'm going to get my weekly to-do list done, but I consistently fail at doing so and nothing happens to me, then I'm not likely to change my behavior because no one has called me out on it. When poor performance becomes acceptable, it can spread through your business like a cancer and eventually kill it.

Team members should hold each other to account for things as simple and basic as starting a meeting on time. Being late to formation in the morning is a big deal in the military, and it should be the same in your company.

If you're late for my meeting, you'll get the first taste of my Business Sergeant mentality. It's extremely disrespectful for the team when everyone else is on time and one person isn't. At one business I was coaching the new sales leader showed up 20 minutes late when the rest of us had gotten there 20 minutes early. He was blaming the weather and the traffic and everything else except for himself. In front of the entire leadership team, I let him have it: "Being late is bad enough, but when you don't take any responsibility for it, shame on you!"

Later, after he was fired for not selling ANYTHING in six months, his team said to me, "He 100% deserved that!" And my reply was, "Why didn't anyone say that to him before?" I was fired up, and looked at the rest of the team and asked, "Who else was thinking that he needed that?" Boom—all hands went up!

In the same way, if a team member shows up to a weekly meeting without something important completed from their to-do list, that person should be called out in public, respectfully but directly.

The only way to execute on agreements and commitments is by being accountable to each other. Remember—an employee who lacks accountability usually lacks respect for himself and/or for others.

Accountability is often in short supply in the business world because people aren't willing to hold one another accountable—even when they're sitting in the owner's box or working inside the leadership team. It doesn't matter what your last name is or your rank in the organization; you're either accountable or you're not. Your leadership team has to lead by example. Just as you can't be "kind of" pregnant, you can't be "kind of" accountable. You either are or you aren't.

LESSON 36 ★ Have Clear Standards and Consequences for Poor Performance

Business leaders—even good ones—get overwhelmed and take people or things for granted, so you have to be consistent with what you expect of your people, especially your mid-managers. According to the *Wall Street Journal*, "The best workplaces are built on clear expectations and candid feedback. In such a workplace firing may be unpleasant, but it won't be a shock. And often poor performing workers will read the writing on the wall and leave or find another job before a firing becomes necessary."

I like to ask the teams I work with, "please explain to me what the consequences are when employees don't hit their numbers. What's the plan? Do you have a process for every possible contingency? Do you have specific consequences for the first infraction, the second infraction, the third infraction? Do you have a three-strike rule?" Not having that kind of clear context is a failure of management.

That was the problem at 303 Software, which we discussed at the end of chapter one: a failure of management in enforcing accountability. As Matt Jaffe, the company's CEO, recalls:

> When people were delegated tasks, they didn't have responsibility for completing them. We had this idea that we called tag-teaming, where if you need to get something done, a couple people would work on it together, but nobody was actually accountable and nobody was delegating. We had a really flat structure before Chris, pretty much everybody reported to me and Stefan, so there was no accountability in terms of a reporting structure. Things would never get done and people would say, "Oh, I was working on it with so and so, and that person got too busy, so we didn't finish the project."
>
> Now you can't say that. If you have a task delegated to you, you own it. That person can then delegate that task to people further down the chain or laterally, but the ownership of the task doesn't change. It remains with the person it was originally delegated to. We never operated with that concept before.

Responsibility and ownership are now part of our values and that has made a huge change in our company.

We lost some people when we changed direction because they liked the old way when they weren't held accountable for anything. They liked collecting a paycheck and not having any responsibility. But Chris's tough-love approach has totally turned around our culture and for the most part people are much happier. And I can certainly measure how much more productive we are. We were able to transform our company from one that was on the brink of bankruptcy to one that is now profitable, growing, and a happy place to come to work every day.

Lots of talk and no action always equals much lower levels of accountability, because the only way for us to execute on a regular basis is to be accountable to each other. If we don't have that accountability to each other—*or the client*—if somebody's not counting on us to get it done, I've found in my experience we're usually a little less motivated to get it done. To avoid this, it's very important for team members to become accountability partners when necessary. Holding one another accountable and executing on a daily basis is the lifeblood of a healthy company, and it's once again very, very difficult without a business operating system.

It's so easy to be fired up about one part of your business, then all of a sudden this part catches fire and you literally have to shuffle priorities. However, when you have an operating system, at least then you have an order in which you're going to work on priorities, how you're going to work on them, what "done" looks like, etc. So when you have a system to align and synchronize all the moving parts of your business, you can track who's doing what and when it needs to get done by. If you don't have a system, how do you know what's getting done and what isn't?

LESSON 37 ★ Create an Action Plan for Employee Improvement

You also need to create an action plan for improvement so you can hold that troubled employee accountable if he/she doesn't improve. When you set the standards, the employees either understand where the performance bar sits or they do not. If they do, then it's their job to meet them; if they can't meet them, then you need to find others who can. It's as simple as that. It's a problem when the tough conversation is more uncomfortable for you than employees not performing to expectations.

As a Business Sergeant, you need to have clarity that your company's standards are consistently being met. If everything is out in the open and an employee just doesn't meet the standards, you need to give that employee 60 days to correct the problem. A lot of companies say 90 days, but in my experience their heart really isn't in it if they haven't fixed it within 60. If they're sincere about changing, they'll usually make changes within the first 30 days. If they don't, you might as well help them transition out to go find the unit that fits them, because yours is clearly not the one.

LESSON 38 ★ Don't Alienate the A Players

If you're a part of a team and you set a deadline for getting something done, then either as a team member or leader you can pretty much set your watch on it. Enjoying consistently high levels of discipline in execution comes from a history of expecting and managing your team to high levels of discipline in accountability. If you're on a team that's very accountable to each other and you all are operating at a high standard, then a lack of accountability will be very frustrating to those "A players." The culture the team has created won't tolerate an inferior level of performance or accountability, because when you naturally have it and when you are forced to work with others who don't, its demotivating to your A players. When you as a Business Sergeant don't enforce that standard company-wide, it puts your A players in a very difficult spot, and it might even make them less accountable if they start asking, "why should I even try?" In my experience, the A players will become C players way before the C players become A players.

Once that slowdown begins, A players will question why they should work at a company that allows C player behavior. This can have a ripple effect on the health of your business: those big priorities aren't getting accomplished with the same intensity of commitment, execution, and accountability. And that's when you stop being an elite unit. A true A player is not going to stand for it and will go find another team of A players to soldier with. You might be wondering what a B player is? My definition of that is simply, someone who has "A" qualities, but displays enough "C" performance that we're not comfortable giving them the "A" player title. "B" players are much harder to spot than "C" players; that's why they are so dangerous in a small business setting!

A players don't just show up for the big plays; they understand that the little day-to-day things not getting done can add up real quick and create huge issues that eventually become hard to unravel. So it's important for a Business

Sergeant to remember that it's the little stuff that requires accountability across the board.

Remember throughout this process that while real accountability in the office is rare, it's very powerful when you achieve it. Attaining that accountability may be challenging and require continuous pushing before you get traction going, but once you do, that passion can fuel the fire for you. A players want to be on the field of business battle with other A players who push them to be the best they can be.

They're often too afraid to tell you they're losing faith or direction or commitment or passion because they're disappointed in you for NOT stepping up in your role. If you're too weak to stand up to your weakest links, then take the title off your business card now, because it's not fair to your people. If you disappoint them long enough, they'll leave in search of a stronger team with a stronger coach. But when you become the strong and capable guiding hand they want you to be, and they see you're really invested in them, then that's when the magic happens. That's when the team rallies from behind and pulls out a victory. Once you've not just benched but cut from the squad those who don't want to be challenged, who don't want to be accountable, who are content with mediocrity at your expense, you'll see immediate returns on your investment in excellence. Your job as a great leader is to spark the growth in your team and keep challenging and developing them at all times.

LESSON 39 ★ Always Keep Score

A scorecard goes by many names—a flash report, a KPI (Key Performance Indicator) a dashboard, or a metric. There are probably a hundred terms for giving somebody a number to rate performance. A lot of businesses don't use a scorecard. They try one, it doesn't work for them, and they abandon it. It's a big mistake. A scorecard is crucial if you want accountability in your organization. Whatever scoring system you use, you need to give your employees a number they have to achieve on a weekly basis.

If you have ten people in the processing department, and they all have similar titles and pay and areas of responsibility, one of them is going to out-produce the others. One of them is going to be first and one is going to be last. Once you start using a scorecard, you'll be able to identify quickly who's committed and properly trained and who is not.

A scorecard will tell you who owns a particular task, the goal of that task, and how successful completion of the task is measured. The beauty of a scorecard is that you don't have to do daily micromanagement of your employees. Everyone has a weekly number they're responsible for. They understand that if they have a light Monday, Tuesday is going to have to be a little busier. If you track patterns and trends only on a monthly basis, you could miss unhealthy behavior for quite some time. Monitoring people on a weekly basis allows you to see and address problems much more quickly and proactively, whether it's a training issue or a commitment issue.

Too many companies spend a lot of time and money researching the past versus the present or the future. If you develop a great scorecard and are smart in using it, it will help you see a little bit into the future and avoid surprises. For instance, if you're an online retailer and your web traffic is booming for days on end, you should probably call the factory and get an extra run started before you need it. If your volume is up, you'll need more products on the shelves.

A weekly scorecard helps you to maintain discipline daily. And if you look at an employee's performance over the whole week and the numbers are off, what conversation are you prepared to have with the person who is accountable for that number? What performance improvement plan do you have waiting?

In having that conversation, you also have to be prepared to hold yourself or a member of your team accountable as well. If you find out that someone wasn't trained or supervised properly, or didn't receive the right resources, you need to take responsibility for that, apologize and take corrective measures. In having a conversation about accountability, it's rarely just about the employee. It's another mirror moment to look at your role in creating the problem. I've often seen business leaders get really frustrated with their people, but when I dig down a bit, it's usually the leaders themselves who have failed the employees and they don't even see it. You have to be super alert in avoiding that kind of sloppy leadership.

A players love scorecards, while "B" and "C" players not so much, as it validates their less–than "A" status. They may think they're an A player, but a measurable accountability metric is something they can't argue with. Once you get everyone to see the negative results of a lack of accountability by painting a vivid picture of all the pain it causes, and show them how easily that pain is avoided with some common goals and a little community policing, everyone should come on board. They will help you root out the weak links through their shared commitment to keeping the bar consistently high.

LESSON 40 ★ Create a 90 day world™ and use Rocks

Being an effective Business Sergeant requires consistently setting clear and achievable goals to accomplish on a weekly basis, leading up to the quarter and beyond, all the way to your long term 5- to 30-years-out big, inspiring goal that provides energy and context for your journey together. You absolutely should be thinking that far ahead in your vision as it sets the context for everybody.

Then you can then drill down to a Three-Year Picture™, and work your way back to a One-Year Plan™ and then to the Quarterly Rocks. You need weekly scorecards to get there, because most people have no more than a 90-day attention span. Some others like me, have a much shorter attention span, so be careful not to exceed this 90-day time-frame. Exceeding it can lead to frayed alignment, relationships, and focus. A similar military term for this is mission creep, where without detailed and focused mission planning with regular check-ins, you find yourself conducting another mission altogether, and that of course can be problematic. To combat this, another thing we teach our clients in the EOS process™ is to create a 90-Day World™ to laser-focus your team. After 90 days, dust them off, re-focus, and re-center them. Give them a pat on the back or a kick in the butt, whichever is appropriate, and then get them fired-up for the next quarter by sharing new strategic priorities (Rocks). Show them what the new Rocks will do for the company once completed.

Rocks, a term borrowed from leadership and management legend Dr. Stephen Covey, is a strategic initiative outside of your normal day-to-day way of doing things that can really grow the business. It may be a new capability, a new capacity, that bolt-of-lightning idea or product or new system that makes you better. Another example might be taking someone who's junior in the organization and putting them in a position of authority and responsibility and accountability by making them the Rock "Owner".

You make the "kid" the project leader and you get to learn new things because they're going approach the problem in an entirely different way. That young person leading can also get mentorship and guidance from those following, and you get to develop your employees in new ways. I always recommend that my clients do something unexpected. Put someone in charge who you wouldn't normally select. Clients have done that and gotten some unique and impressive results.

If you're not improving your business, you're just maintaining it. Actually, you're going backwards while your competitors are improving their businesses. People like to check off five, six, seven, or eight things that they've done, relatively insignificant things, and then go home and feel good about it, but they didn't really substantially change a damn thing about the company.

You should probably devote 20% of your time outside of simply operating in the day-to-day. This is when you have the chance to find a new supplier, create a new process, bring in a new product, to create a capability that you didn't have before.

By calling it a Rock, we've acknowledged this isn't in our day-to-day, but we all need to work on it simultaneously while executing the day-to-day. You're upgrading your business while you're doing business. Covey's whole point is this: if you pick just a handful of things each quarter to work on versus 40 things, you got a great chance of getting five or six of those things done to a masterful level, rather than getting 40 things done at a half-assed level.

My most successful clients are the ones who pick four or five things to accomplish and then masterfully execute those four or five things. And they do that every quarter. Because they're so good at executing, they're creating new significant capabilities with their organizations. Companies that try to achieve too much (or too little) are just spinning their wheels. Rocks are a way to say, "let's get focused and be really intentional."

If you're smart, you can figure out what your big goal is in 3 or 10 years, and then you basically just create successive Rocks to get there. Some things have to be done and in place before other things, but you can plan strategically about how you're going to eat that elephant one bite (one quarter) at a time.

With clients, I check out the Rocks that I helped them establish in the previous quarter. Did we execute them at 80% or better? Did we get the majority of them done? We don't expect perfection, but we do expect progress. If they don't get most of them done, we have a somewhat uncomfortable accountability conversation so they can learn from their mistakes and not repeat them. The point is, if you failed to get the Rocks done in 90 days, it doesn't mean that the initiative's going to fail. You'll get those Rocks done in the first weeks of the next quarter. Again, the best teams get them all done, so they now have the bandwidth and headspace to pick new things and go after them without having to worry about finishing up the old ones.

It's a continual improvement process. And when they get it right, they celebrate being a great company and executing well.

You set expectations high by creating laser-focused, crystal-clear weekly goals. You don't pick a number out of the sky that you've never hit. You pick a number you know is hittable. Once you hit that standard, we then raise the standard to accommodate the next level of progress. And once we achieve that, we ratchet it up further.

It's just like going to the gym. You don't start with 300 pounds on the bench. You start with maybe 150 pounds, and you rep that for a little bit. You warm up your muscles. As you continue training, you keep adding more weight to the bar.

It's the same thing with performance expectations. We want an elite performance but not an unrealistic one—a level of performance that's highly profitable and that's good for the company, but that also respects the employees. We don't want to grind people down or wear them out. We want a healthy blend between productivity, profitability and employee morale.

Once you find that sweet spot, then it's just a process managing everyone to stay in that spot, that optimal range for your business.

When you have these metrics and they're super-measurable, people either meet the standards or they don't. It becomes a black-and-white way to hold each team member accountable, taking all the wishy-washy gray out of it. Without a scorecard, you're just going on feeling, and it's very difficult to hold people accountable based on perceptions. But it's very easy to hold people accountable to a scorecard number that's either on or off track. If you want an open and honest culture, a scorecard is a great step in that direction. Without such a tool, bringing discipline and accountability into your organization is very difficult, but with one, you have a fighting chance.

The bottom line is that accountability is a lot more fun when we're all doing it together; it really is a team sport. When you have accountability teammates, you're building trust in the process of keeping each other on the right track. Encouraging that kind of culture in your company is the best way to avoid having to fire anyone, but when you do have to take that step, remember you're doing it for the benefit of your entire team. I'm a firm believer that anything that can be easily measured can be easily managed, and that accountability is never a dirty word. Accountability to our core values, to our culture, to our business results, and ultimately to ourselves is what business leadership is all about.

FOCUS ON THE CLIENT
Committing to Accountability at Zenman

Keith Roberts, the founder of Zenman, a full-service digital marketing agency, is a very talented man—a high-level graphic artist, photographer, and digital marketer. He was committed to having a great office and to getting the right clients, and he did all that without having the right infrastructure, the right leaders, the right levels of accountability, and the right financial controls. Basically, his hobby had turned into a job which then turned into a business. He was committed to doing great work, but by his own admission he wasn't committed to running a business.

Zenman wasn't making payroll when they decided to meet with me. No one, including Keith, had a clue about what was going on. They didn't have any sales in the pipeline, and would be out of cash and payroll in a couple of days. None of the systems in place were working. Communication was poor. They had all kinds of wrong people in the wrong seats. No one was being held accountable.

If you don't have accountability, commitment is a really tricky thing. If you're not willing to be accountable, it's really hard to commit to each other. There was a fear of having tough conversations. If something went wrong that required a difficult conversation, they wouldn't have it. No one got the message that they had to change their ways of working. They were afraid that somebody might get upset or might quit, which is crazy because so many people were in the wrong seats.

It was just really bleak on all levels. Zenman was recognized in the industry for producing great, award-winning work, but couldn't make payroll. It was really shocking to see that Keith was such an expert in one aspect of the business and such a novice on the other. So my work with Zenman revolved around committing the company to accountability.

Let's hear Keith Roberts tell the story:

> *The thing that was broken in my company, and to be honest with you I didn't know why, was profitability. We had a great reputation, we did outstanding work, but we had this business that did well over a million dollars a year but wasn't making money at the end of the year. The only reason the business survived was because when push came to shove, I would just work harder. I would put in 120-hour weeks and sank money into the business.*

I was just a stubborn SOB for lack of a better term—failure was not an option.

My brother was in the #2 seat and I trusted him with finance and the employees, but he wasn't qualified for the position. It was a very unhealthy, actually a toxic relationship that became a cancer in the company. We had other staffing problems we didn't know about. When we started I make the analogy that we were embracing this approach like a drug addict going to rehab who knew if he didn't surrender to the process, he would be dead.

We had a hell of a road in front of us, but it was comforting to know that we had a plan to turn things around.

Before we started, we didn't have core values as a company. We established the concept of accountability based on core values. In our first session it was clear that we needed to do an Accountability Chart™.

After we discovered our core values, we implemented the People Analyzer™ tool from EOS® where you rate each employee for their core value fit within the organization and very clearly outlined expectations: "This is what it takes to work here, this is not a for-fun organization, we're a business." The expectation was that if you don't embody our core values, you don't work here. For the first time, everybody understood the repercussions: "If you don't meet these standards, there's no place on this bus for you."

In our second session, using the People Analyzer™ tool we had to rate ourselves and everybody on our leadership team for both core value fit and if they GWC'd the seat they were going to sit in on the Accountability Chart™. GWC™ stands for if they got their role, wanted to do their role, and if they had the capacity to do their role. My brother basically said, "I get it. I have the capacity to do it, but this isn't the job for me. It's a paycheck, not a passion." He had literally signed his resignation letter. Right after he said that Chris said, "Your W sucks for the finance seat, we'll need to either find you a new role, or you'll have to go." Because we were now able to be very clear and up front about our requirements and expectations, he moved on to a new job that was much better suited to his talents and qualifications.

Now we're much faster to resolve the wrong hire. We had to fire our director of business development when he didn't meet his goals; in the past it would have taken months or even years to do that. And the next person who doesn't meet their sales goals for two quarters is gone. So our tolerance for non-performance is much lower.

One of the things that came out of this was Caitlyn being promoted from project manager to CEO of the business. We had a rock star on the team but she wasn't in the right leadership seat. EOS gave us a system for putting the right people in the right seats, based on their strengths. That's been the most powerful and quantifiable change for me. Caitlyn is a good integrator who shares in my vision. We had eight people on our leadership team, but now we have four. Caitlyn and I are the only two remaining from the original team. In the last two years there's probably been a 75% turnover with our staff, but in a very healthy way.

Promoting Caitlyn to CEO was a major step forward for Zenman. If you define accountability as making sure the trains run on time, then you need to hire someone like Caitlyn to do that. When Keith did this, he was then free to get out of her way, and the company's culture of accountability changed as result.

Let's hear Caitlyn give her view of how the company was transformed:

A few years ago, Zenman was in a growth stage and about to get really big, but weren't quite sure how to do it. We had a lot of procedural issues, cash flow issues, and Keith, our founder, knew we needed some help.

So, Chris came in and met with the leadership team and presented the EOS 90 Minute Meeting™. The concepts seemed really useful, but I thought there was no way it was going to work. There were a few people in leadership positions that shouldn't have been there, and I felt we were merely going to scoot over all the real problems as we had done in the past. Little did I know that Chris would help us totally revolutionize our business and the way we did business from day to day.

By the fourth meeting—which I believe was our first quarterly planning session—we had gotten rid of most of the leadership team. They self-selected and left the organization after realizing from the EOS People Analyzer™ tool that they didn't have the capacity or interest for their role.

The EOS Accountability Chart™ was very helpful in determining people's specific roles and responsibilities. That resulted in major changes in our leadership team and firing our entire sales team. It also resulted in me getting significantly more responsibility. I had always kind of been in that role, but now it was official.

At first it was really rough to start again with a new team in place of one that had been around for 18 years. We had some dark hours there. We had vendors who were demanding to be paid. At one point we didn't have $200 to replace our printer's ink cartridge. We had just fired our whole sales team and had to build an entirely new one. But ultimately we were able to create a committed team that is rolling in the same direction.

When we let go of our director of business development, I said to Keith, "Here's the deal—a year ago we wouldn't have fired him. But now we're slow to hire and quick to fire." So we let him go, suffered the initial pain, but it's an amazing, freeing thing when you get rid of someone who's dragging you down. We ripped off the Band-Aid and are so much better for it.

When I first started working with Keith, I sat down with him for an hour or two. We made up an eight- to ten-point list of the most uncomfortable things in the world he had to do: fire certain people, cancel the orders for new furniture, renegotiate leases, say no to all spending for the next year. I told Keith, "chances are this isn't going to work and you're going to lose the business, but if you do all ten of these things and do them immediately, you might have a chance to make it.

Within a week or two, Keith crossed everything off that list. I've never seen anybody so committed to execution. That's when I knew he had a chance. And they have turned it around. They're no longer losing money every month and they're planning for a profit this year. In fact, in two years' time, Zenman has made a tremendous turn around, as they were just named the top digital marketing company in Denver by Colorado Business magazine, and they are working with some pretty well known brands, hitting it out of the park with the quality of their work—and their balance sheet is looking pretty darn good as well.

EOS ACCOUNTABILITY CHART™

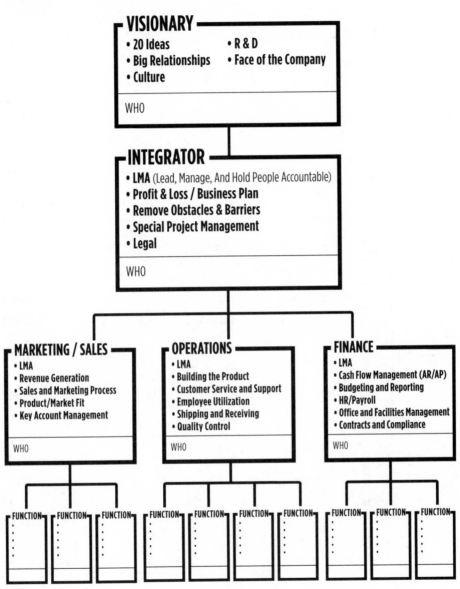

VISIONARY
- 20 Ideas
- Big Relationships
- Culture
- R & D
- Face of the Company

WHO

INTEGRATOR
- **LMA** (Lead, Manage, And Hold People Accountable)
- **Profit & Loss / Business Plan**
- **Remove Obstacles & Barriers**
- **Special Project Management**
- **Legal**

WHO

MARKETING / SALES
- LMA
- Revenue Generation
- Sales and Marketing Process
- Product/Market Fit
- Key Account Management

WHO

OPERATIONS
- LMA
- Building the Product
- Customer Service and Support
- Employee Utilization
- Shipping and Receiving
- Quality Control

WHO

FINANCE
- LMA
- Cash Flow Management (AR/AP)
- Budgeting and Reporting
- HR/Payroll
- Office and Facilities Management
- Contracts and Compliance

WHO

FUNCTION · · · ·   FUNCTION · · · ·   FUNCTION · · · ·   FUNCTION · · · ·   FUNCTION · · · ·   FUNCTION · · · ·   FUNCTION · · · ·   FUNCTION · · · ·   FUNCTION · · · ·   FUNCTION · · · ·

COMPANY SCORECARD

WHO	MEASURABLES	GOAL	5-Jan	12-Jan	19-Jan	26-Jan	2-Feb	9-Feb	16-Feb	23-Feb	1-Mar	8-Mar	15-Mar	22-Mar	29-Mar

EOS®
Entrepreneurial Operating System®

Toolbox

CHAPTER SIX
Marketing & Branding

Consider the following statistics on businesses that don't put enough time or thought into honing their brand:

**50%**
of companies
are using digital marketing but they don't have a plan![27]
(SmartInsights.com)

According to *INC* magazine,

IN 2016 ONLY
32%
OF MARKETERS
had a documented content strategy.[28]

The *Harvard Business Review* audited 2,241 U.S. companies, measuring how long each took to respond to a web-generated test lead.[29]

Although 37% responded to their lead within an hour and 16% responded within one to 24 hours, 24% took more than 24 hours—*and 23% of the companies never responded at all!* The average response time, among companies that responded within 30 days, was 42 hours.

According to Forbes, **a majority (60%) of B2B marketers'** challenge is producing engaging content, 57% say measuring content effectiveness is their greatest challenge, and 57% say producing content consistently is their biggest struggle.[30]

It looks like we're clearly in the need for some Business Sergeant lessons about marketing and branding!

[27] http://www.smartinsights.com/internet-marketing-statistics/2015-digital-marketing-stats-the-good-the-bad-and-the-intriguing
[28] https://www.inc.com/sujan-patel/10-statistics-about-content-marketing-in-2016-you-won-t-believe.html
[29] https://hbr.org/2011/03/the-short-life-of-online-sales-leads
[30] https://www.forbes.com/sites/jaysondemers/2015/12/10/35-content-marketing-statistics-you-need-to-know-in-2016

LESSON 41 ★ Market in the Year You Live In

It's vital that you follow the advice of marketing whiz Gary Vaynerchuk, who shares the sage wisdom that you should "market in the year you live in." Fifteen years ago, a full-page ad in the Yellow Pages meant you had a steady supply of leads; today it's almost all digital in nature. Sure, there are some other mediums you can use depending on your business—outbound marketing/cold calling/mailers. But you have to be running the right type of business for those more archaic methods to still be effective.

Compare the old with the new; for instance, the conversion rate for cold calls has dropped like a stone in recent years because that's simply not how people enjoy being marketed to. Inc. magazine sounded the alarm in 2016 that "content marketing isn't being leveraged nearly enough. 57% of B2B marketers are still using print and other offline promotions to market their products and services, despite the fact that only 31% see it as effective."[31]

In today's marketing world, consumers have changed: they're more educated, skeptical, aware of tactics, and really look for testimonials from others users like themselves along with celebrity and influencer endorsements of the products they buy and use. In today's climate, it's really critical for any new or established company to create a strong brand to market their products or services.

Consider *Forbes* magazine's advice: "When you think about your brand, think about all the elements: promise, personality, look, voice, service, attributes, memorability, even patina."[32] With the shift in traditional trends, more and more marketing today is inbound: putting content out there that aligns with people's wants and needs. This means becoming a thought leader, telling people rather than selling them, which resonates much better with the modern consumer.

According to a recent joint study by Nielsen and Google, more than 50% of consumers want to **make a purchase within one hour** of conducting research on their smartphones. That means when they do contact you, typically they're ready to do business. They may have a few questions they still need answered, but they are close to making the transaction and it usually goes quickly. So where outbound marketing used to be King, inbound marketing is now King. The *Huffington Post* notes, "B2B marketing has transformed in recent years thanks to the advancement of the internet, largely led by Google's growth, followed by the explosion of social media. As a result, the advantages

[31] https://www.inc.com/sujan-patel/10-statistics-about-content-marketing-in-2016-you-won-t-believe.html
[32] https://www.forbes.com/sites/loisgeller/2012/05/23/a-brand-is-a-specialized

of inbound marketing are numerous, yet a huge number of companies still haven't discovered how to do it right."[33]

So let's go through a quick crash course.

First, you have to have a brand in order to really market what you do. If you don't have an established brand and you're just marketing your company, then you're basically marketing a commodity, a "me too" company. Once you've established a solid brand, and in the formation of that brand have created attractive and memorable differentiators and talking points, then marketing is the act of broadcasting your inbound and outbound marketing messaging, offers, and events. There are a million things you can do in order for people to find you. A modern day version of that is to have a multi-faceted online and offline strategy, to find the best possible prospects for your business.

Over half the searches for businesses are on smart phones[34], so people are highly mobile and geo-locating services can attract local "walk-in business". When you go to a website and view a product, that product follows you around on the internet in the form of pop up and banner ads also known as retargeting. That technology has been around a while, and the good news is that it's become much more affordable for small business owners to access it now vs. the old days of only larger companies being able to afford those types of marketing tools and technology. For a new start-up, not in a position to spend big money, you have the freedom to test your ideas at a smaller scale and throw it all at the wall and see what sticks. With using small test campaigns using trial and error, you can effectively find the right messaging that attracts a larger amount of customers, and once you've found it, you can go big and maximize your marketing dollars. This can be done in every industry so have some fun and break all the old rules. You have to be patient with a marketing campaign because I've seen people throw in the towel right before something was about to pop. So my advice is go as BIG AS YOU CAN once you've cracked the code.

Make sure the marketing medium you select makes sense from a Return On Investment standpoint when you spend your dollars. For instance, billboards can still make sense for some companies, but if you're a small business, you have to find your customers as cheaply as possible to preserve some margin and create profits for your organization. So in the modern age, digital marketing comes first, followed by the traditional avenues: print, TV, radio, cable, infomercials, trade shows, pop-ups, promotions, event sponsorships,

[33] http://www.huffingtonpost.com/young-entrepreneur-council/5-keys-for-successful-inb_b_11332882.html
[34] http://hitwise.connexity.com/070116_MobileSearchReport_CD_US.html

charitable giving, auctions, tournaments, and sporting events. And that's just a few, because there are a ton of things you can do to let people know who you are and how you can help them.

But understand that you've got to have a crystal clear message of how you can help them and why they should choose you, otherwise your message will be lost in all the other marketing messages people get bombarded with every day.

LESSON 42 ★ Create a Well-Defined Brand

The key to standing out from the white noise is to create a brand that differentiates your business from being a simple commodity. Start by asking the basic question: "Why should someone buy from me?" No one will care about your business unless you can answer that question truthfully and accurately. Chances are great that you don't have 100% market share. Your goal, then, is to try and capture as much of that market share as you can. If you can differentiate your brand by creating a richer experience than your competitors and for a similar price point, the consumer is going to choose your business again and again.

If you're the type of business that has repeat customers, that's the difference between flourishing and hardly making payroll, which is the entire argument in business. So when I say, "create a brand," we're really talking about your identity and your culture, because culture defines your personal identity and your company's DNA and that's really your brand. It's really powerful when all of that shines through from the inside and moves consumers to embrace your product or service!

Marketing whiz Gary Vaynerchuk, in addition to recommending that you, "market in the year you live in," also recommends that you "understand the emerging markets, understand where your consumer is, and meet them there. Don't make them come to you."[35] Frame your marketing priorities around the trends that work for your competitors.

When you have a really well-defined brand, marketing is so much easier. Your product or service makes sense, it attracts people, it's well constructed. Too often, companies create a tagline that says: "Honest, Trustworthy, Quality Service." Not exactly original. Come on— you're spending money to say same thing everyone else is saying? That's *NOT* smart marketing! You need to get to know your customers as well as your own company, which starts with nailing

[35] https://www.garyvaynerchuk.com/marketing-in-the-year-2016

down the basics:

- Who are your ideal customers? Who do you serve the best?

- Where do you make the most profit?

- Who do you enjoy working with?

- What are your customers looking for? What product or service are they seeking?

- What need in the market are you filling? What demand are you satisfying?

- What is your desired result for delivery of that product or service to the client?

- How will you continue to add value to their lives?

Lastly, what's your *why?* Your customer should understand *why* you want to do it better than the competition. If they have to drive further to get to you, what are you doing right to make them drive that far? How can you get them to give you repeat business and tell their friends about you?

So first figure out who you're building your company for, because it's a problem if you don't know who your target market is. Next, give credence to one of my favorite business quotes in the world, from the great e-commerce guru Jeff Bezos, CEO of Amazon.com: "Branding is what people say when you're not around." You want buzz like, "Oh, you have to call my stock guy!" or "Hey, you won't believe my dentist, that was the most stress free root canal I've ever had!"

To use a military metaphor, you have to know where you're pointing your weapon. This is often what I ask a new team I'm working with: "What the heck are you aiming at?!" If you want to earn your Expert Qualification badge in marketing, you have to be laser-focused on promoting your service and knowing why the consumer should want to return to you over and over again.

Forbes magazine offers this cautionary advice that you should put on a sticky-note somewhere on your desk: "It takes a lot of time, money, and very hard work to build and maintain great brands like that, brands that can speak volumes in just a few syllables."[36] Remember those words: *time, money,* and *very hard work.*

So it's key that you keep an ear to the street about the buzz around your brand, your reputation, and your story. The modern consumer wants to know *WHY* you do what you do even more than *what* you do. This is why we put a spotlight on defining your company brand, and the experience a consumer

[36] https://www.forbes.com/sites/loisgeller/2012/05/23/a-brand-is-a-specialized

has when they interact with your business. Most businesses are commodities-based and provide something a lot of other companies do, so in order to stand out and be remarkable, you have to make the consumer's experience simply better. You have to be very deliberate in how you do that, with systems and core values and employees who really want to execute to a high standard.

The average customer obviously wants to work with the best company offering the best value, and highest quality at the lowest possible price. That combination will ALWAYS be your consumer equation. I know this can be annoying to a business owner, but it's the way of the world in sales. So my motto has always been: Show your customer how they will get more value from you for the same or less money than others, and you'll win BIG in sales.

It's obviously more complicated than it sounds, but messaging should always be simple in marketing, as should the service follow-through of that messaging when you're dealing with a customer. You'll be successful if you can be consistent on both ends of that spectrum as a business owner or marketing decision maker, because there are PLENTY of customers out there waiting to be serviced. And quite often they're waiting not because they don't have the money to spend, but because they're trying to make sure your messaging is equal to your actual follow-through on the customer service end (along with, of course, the quality of the product or service you're selling).

LESSON 43 ★ Go Guerrilla in Your Marketing Tactics

Another theme I drive home in my coaching is that marketing and branding are NOT the same thing and are too often confused as being so. Your brand is the key to unlocking consumer interest, from how your product or service makes them feel, to how they talk about your brand afterward to other potential customers. How you MARKET that BRAND is what determines how successful your business will be—it's that simple. If you don't have any leads, you don't have any sales; if you don't have any sales, you don't have any customers; if you don't have any customers, you don't have a business.

Now, if you find yourself in the rare position of having more sales than you can handle, that's again what I like to call a First World problem and a good one to have, vs. not having enough sales to cover your overhead, which we call a Third World problem.

I highly recommend implementing guerrilla marketing tactics as much as conventional ones too, because as long as it's not illegal or immoral, it's okay with the Business Sergeant—including on the recruiting front. My point is, it doesn't matter what you are marketing for, whether it's for customers or top talent for your business. When I was running my own construction company and marketing for new top tier sales reps, I would create one-page flyers that were pretty compelling based on information I had about the business I was targeting. Then I would paper my competitors' parking lots when I knew they had a sales meeting that day. This was pretty bold, and I got some angry phone calls, but it was how I wound up hiring some of my best sales producers—I found them right in the parking lot of their employer, or I'd meet them at a tradeshow that we both attended, or I'd have them come and give an estimate at my home, or a friend or family member's home and see how they did.

I realize that's really, really aggressive, but that's the attitude you need to the best of the best in marketing your brand to consumers or potential "A" player employees. Are you willing to go all-in? Are you able to come up with ideas to market your brand that beat your competitors? To think like a Business Sergeant means being strategic in fighting the war for the almighty sale, while applying the military credo of *Improvise, Adapt, and Overcome.* Some of the coolest things that work great are not the usual conventional tools. So don't be afraid to try new things that go against the grain.

LESSON 44 ★ Marketing Isn't Sales

Don't make the mistake, as so many business owners and leaders do, of co-mingling your sales and marketing departments. Don't assume that someone who's an expert at closing sales is also an expert at generating the leads they're closing. Those are two entirely separate functions. When I ran other entrepreneurs' sales and marketing departments as an executive—and when I owned my own businesses—one of the most important lessons I learned was the importance of compartmentalizing each of those functions within your business. If you don't have the expertise in both, bring in an expert employee or hire a strategic partner who has the expertise, so you can focus on what you're good at, and both will be done to a higher level and complement each other.

You begin by making sure your brand is clearly defined to both your sales and marketing teams before it ever reaches the consumer. Your brand has to be established to do effective marketing, but there are plenty of people marketing without a good brand. Let's be clear, you can do #2 without #1, so let's not confuse the two and understand that branding is a separate function from marketing. It's really rare that a company is exceptional at both; they're separate and distinct art forms, and when you compartmentalize them it's easier to find out what works and what doesn't. Marketing is about generating leads, not selling them, while sales is about taking those leads and sending your sales team into the field to sell your company's brand and product.

Leads and sales revenues are the oxygen and blood of your business; you'll bleed out if you don't have customers to talk to and things to sell them. That's Captain Obvious talking here, but when you have consistent lead flow, you can respond to the market accordingly. If you don't, you can wind up over-promising and under–delivering, and that's your sales reputation you're playing with. By the same token, if you don't have leads and people to talk to, even if you do have a good product or service, you'll go out of business and be back to selling for somebody else, while you dig yourself out of a huge hole.

So having a steady flow of leads and knowing how to turn them up and down is the puzzle you have to solve as a business owner. Otherwise, panic and anxiety will set in and wreak havoc on your personal and professional lives. If you're not sleeping well, you can't bring 100% to the war room every day and provide the leadership your troops need to head onto the business battlefield. If they sense weakness in you, they won't be fired up to follow you; if you give off what I like to call the "wounded animal scent," your employees and clients will sense the desperation because it's not sweet-smelling cologne.

Rightsizing your marketing budget is crucial as well. Some businesses require quite a bit, while other people have a smaller marketing budget because the business is more referral-based or location-based. So there's a wide spectrum in determining your marketing budget. When you have a higher profit margin, for instance, you're probably going to have a higher percentage marketing spend; if you have a lower margin, then an increase in marketing expense or a lack of leads or sales conversions can drain your pockets very quickly. So it's very important to know your numbers, your break-even points, and what your business objectives are. And it's all about the numbers at the end of the year, not for any single time period during that year.

This is where the beauty of scorecards comes into play. According to the *Harvard Business Review,* even though "today's managers recognize the impact that measures have on performance… they rarely think of measurement as an essential part of their strategy… the balanced scorecard provides executives with a comprehensive framework that translates a company's strategic objectives into a coherent set of performance measures. Much more than a measurement exercise, the balanced scorecard is a management system that can motivate breakthrough improvements in such critical areas as product, process, customer, and market development."[37]

The brilliance of a scorecard number is that everyone is accountable to it. You have to give your marketing department scorecard numbers because there has to be a metric to hold them accountable. If you're spending money and not getting any customers, it will be directly correlated in the metrics. Without a tracking system, you'll never know. A good way to start is with your next event or next offer; simply put a code on the offer/coupon, and when it gets redeemed, record the successful sale in your marketing database. You can then start to track the ROI on your campaigns. With this simple approach, you'll be able to lower your marketing costs and keep your pipeline full.

LESSON 45 ★ Managing Lead Flow

Defining your marketing process and making sure that process will be followed by all is essential for any business owner. This allows you to nail down the procedure for handling inbound calls. Your policy might be to answer the phone no later than the second ring for any inbound call. I've read many studies that show that leads go cold within minutes.

The *Harvard Business Review* qualified this stark reality when they recently released the results of a study involving 1.25 million sales leads received by 29 B2C and 13 B2B companies in the U.S.: "Firms that tried to contact potential customers within an hour of receiving a query were nearly seven times as likely to qualify the lead (which we defined as having a meaningful conversation with a key decision maker) as those that tried to contact the customer even an hour later—and more than 60 times as likely as companies that waited 24 hours or longer."[38]

So it's critical to follow up leads *FAST, FAST, FAST!* The money you're spending on marketing isn't going to payroll or office overhead, so you better make sure it's money well spent. If your clients interact with your brand after business hours, you'll need to staff your email or phone with an onsite or a remote on-call employee to capture them and convert them like a boss.

[37] https://hbr.org/1993/09/putting-the-balanced-scorecard-to-work
[38] https://hbr.org/2011/03/the-short-life-of-online-sales-leads

Managing lead flow is KEY, and if you can't plan your business and staffing complement—i.e., how many people you need to make your sales goals—you add all kinds of organizational complexity to your business that you don't need. I call it the "Rubber Band Effect" because you're always on loading or offloading people, resulting in a bunch of chickens running around with their heads cut off. It's not a lot of fun to have that kind of chaos running wild among your sales staff, so get your act together and make sure you have a consistent lead flow.

So as a business owner, everything has to be systematized to make sure you're serving the client the best way you can. That's what your business makes its money from (to be Captain Obvious again), but it's shocking how many small business owners can lose sight of that simple fact. A great way to bring about systemization is by creating a marketing funnel. There are countless funnels out there, all the way from custom to in-the-box solutions depending on your needs. You can create and run campaigns where your brand is presented in the best possible light. And you don't have to "sell" your customers—when they do their due diligence on the web, you're able to start a conversation with them and provide a solution that is exactly right for their personal or business needs.

When you're creating a campaign of this sort, you need to cast the *personas* correctly. In business-to-business (B2B) marketing, the first is usually the business owner, who has his/her unique set of issues/challenges to identify/relate to in your messaging. Second would be the executives—mid-to-senior team leaders and managers with a lot of responsibility and who have their own set of issues. And finally, their employees, the people on the line who are really making it happen. They're the soldiers in the trenches, so to speak, servicing customers on the front lines, and responsible for promoting/representing their brand and the consumer experience with their company.

For business-to-consumer (B2C) businesses, you can also create personas to market effectively into a household. For example, in one of my construction businesses, I learned that females aged 35 to 65 made the lion's share of decisions regarding home improvements, so my marketing had a softer more aesthetic feel rather than the functional and affordable messaging males are traditionally attracted to.

To manage all those facets effectively as a Business Sergeant, you have to interact with different personas differently on each of those levels, from where the sales relationship begins to where it ends upon execution. It's a natural hand-off if you've got everything running right between the various departments in your company.

In delivering on all that, it's critical to understand that your value as a brand depends on your ability to deliver in the servicing, which many small business owners and leaders lose sight of in this respect: Servicing starts NOT with the final product the customer receives, but with the first interaction the customer has with anyone representing your company, from the initial sale to the final delivery (all of those "Touch Points"). Again, any time you can send out a specific offer and put a code on it, you have an effective way to track where and how your marketing dollars are being spent in giving you the greatest return for your investment. There's an old saying in marketing that's almost always true: "If you can't accurately measure it, you can't accurately manage it."

It's a total package, and when you wrap it up neatly with messaging that resonates with the right person and the right service that follows through, you will inspire word-of-mouth referrals and the sky's the limit. To create a sustainable client-customer eco-system, your job is to treat your first-time customers so well that they immediately become repeat customers and endorse you to others. It's a beautiful thing when you create those kinds of new leads without spending any more money to generate them.

LESSON 46 ★ Don't Be Afraid to Outsource

You need to have a good lead flow within your departments and know exactly how they are affecting your bottom line. Trouble can arise when a business owner doesn't understand the process by which leads are generated (especially in the year 2017! Things have dramatically changed in the last few years). In that scenario, the owner can become strangely dependent on a marketing staff's "expertise" even when, in reality, that expertise doesn't exist. As the business owner, you need to understand exactly how you get leads, but at the same time know who is best to execute those leads, even if you need to go outside your unit to generate the best results for your company and the customers you're serving. Here's the bottom line lesson from the Business Sergeant: don't overpay in-house for what you can outsource. Never be afraid to spend outside of your organization to give your people room to breathe and the chance to excel at their best skill-sets.

You should be courting marketing companies, whether traditional, digital, or a mix of both, to find out what's working with clients in businesses similar to yours. Take each of them out for a test drive, so to speak, and let them sell you on what they can do for you. Find a company who understands your vision and culture, and engage with them because they're the experts. If you don't have a killer internal marketing department, hire a killer outside marketing agency. At the end of the day, you have to be crystal clear on how much money you're going to spend and where you're going to spend it, because not all advertising or marketing is direct response. Track your marketing expenses on a weekly basis to make sure you don't get off course. As the saying goes, "It's not what you make, it's what you keep."

LESSON 47 ★ Always Review and Test

An endlessly effective tool in that tracking results is a military concept called an *After-Action Review.* After an operation or mission, the military has an open and honest discussion about what went well and what didn't go so well. Probe your team to find out what they were thinking and not thinking. Did they remember their training or forget about it? That review process is a really valuable way to find out what worked and what didn't, and how to improve the next time. GREAT brainstorming can come out of this process that helps everybody improve together. Managers can learn better ways to train new sales recruits, while your current sales force can gain insight into what makes a successful sale happen and how to cast your brand in the best light to consumers.

It's also vitally important to "A/B" test your approaches: "Does this work? Or does it not work? Is this cost-effective marketing? Is our branding working?" It's just incredibly important to measure the effect of every dollar. If you're not sure whether it's best to do your outbound marketing in-house or to outsource that function, it might be easier to engage a company that's a subject matter expert in this area. It might make more sense to put your resources in other places, like following up on leads. Or it might be smarter for you to invest in a larger sales force instead of in the marketing department if leads are overflowing.

So, as you step bravely onto the business battlefield to try out new marketing concepts, always begin by asking yourself the age-old question: what's the definition of insanity? The answer: doing the same damned thing over and over again and expecting a different result. Sometimes business owners are afraid to try new things because they're getting something for their effort and are worried they'll lose that. If you have a limited amount of resources to spend on marketing for the purpose of generating new leads, believe me, I totally understand that, but finding the biggest bang for your buck and constantly re-testing things is the best way forward. Your goal is to learn from that experience and share that experience. An after-action review can determine the best ROI, as you learn from the results and move forward.

Building a Great Brand at Pride Energy Solutions

I started my own energy-efficiency remodeling company back in 2009, in the midst of the Great Recession. Most of the companies in that space were going out of business, yet my sales grew to almost $2 million in my first year of business because of my ability to create a brand that had a powerful "why." We weren't just a remodeling company—we were an energy-efficiency company during a time when climate change, America's dependence on foreign oil and the geo-political issues of the Middle East were gaining a lot of national attention while the economy stalled and spending severely slowed—even with those not directly affected by the downturn. Our campaign tapped into the consumer's willingness to do their part as an American by improving energy efficiency, thereby creating energy independence that ultimately addresses the problem of constantly sending America's men and women in our military to the Middle East "Sand Box" to protect our dependent interests, and also stimulating the economy in a meaningful and positive way.

I called the company Pride Energy Solutions, creating a brand my customers could take pride in because they were part of something bigger than themselves. Again, smart marketing was at work here—we understood and fulfilled the consumer's values while at the same time maximizing our own values across branding and marketing fronts. Our product really did make sense—our brand worked because people really got what we stood for and why we were doing it.

I was able to find a key team member, a former Green Peace canvassing (door-to-door appointment setting) manager who was very passionate about the environment. He was able to recruit like-minded people to knock on doors in the cold because they were fired up about our "Greater Good" mission.

We did insulation, doors, windows, and air sealing, the things that really affect the customer's comfort and quality of life in addition to the energy savings. A lot of the homes we worked on had turn-of-the-century construction and were located in cold weather country, so there was a legitimate need for our services.

Lucky for us, there was a good return on investment for remodeling your home even when the real estate market was down, because you could generally get a percentage of it back. So by selling products that were more energy efficient, I could also save homeowners money on their utility costs, make them more comfortable in the process, and give them some resale value. At the same time, these homeowners were helping the environment, which sells itself, so the ROI was greatly accelerated.

If my sales and marketing teams hadn't been passionate about what we were doing, they wouldn't have slogged through frigid weather and risked having doors slammed in their faces. Our marketing had to be "in your face"— we had thirty seconds or less to make our message resonate.

At the time the Federal bailout stimulus was offering a $1,500 tax credit for weatherizing your home, so our sales people could offer a bonus: "This is what the price is, AND here's a $1,500 tax credit, so here's the net cost." Offering a high-performance product at a good price helped us enjoy a solid 50% profit margin on everything we were doing. On top of that, I spent several months putting together a very compelling 15-page booklet for our sales team, a very professional presentation worthy of a much larger company.

Because we had such a different and powerful message, we were able to get traction during a very hard time. Unlike other companies, it was a performance-based culture and I had a brand that enabled me to build a sales team of energetic young people who had a passion for the environment. On top of that, my marketing people who knocked on doors in the dead of winter were all working on commission. I paid 8% of the job to them, the salesperson who closed the sale also got 8%,,and if you did both, you made 16%. When you did well you got a way bigger percentage, and when you didn't, you got nothing, so everyone who chose to work for me had to be highly motivated all around.

Some of them were pulling down $20,000 projects and making big commissions. In some cases I was handing 19-year-old kids $1,600 commission checks after only a few days on the job. Every one of my competitors was going the opposite direction, all because we came up with a powerful brand and a way to market it that provided sustainable and affordable leads

DISCOVERING YOUR BRAND WORKSHEET

Who are you? Are you valuable to them? What will your client & prospective clients say about you when you're not around?

WHO are your "Perfect" or "Favorite" customers to work with? _____

_____

_____

_____

WHAT EXACTLY are they seeking from a service provider, what do they need? What is your logical or emotional solution or approach to make them happy or solve their problem? _____

_____

_____

_____

WHY should they use you vs. countless competitors and refer you to their friends and family again and again? _____

_____

_____

_____

——— CIRCLE ALL THAT APPLY ———

WHO: Why are these your favorite customers?	• Timeline • Expertise • No interest in doing • Their expectations	• Their fears and concerns • How they will make their buying decision • When they will make their buying decision
WHAT: Why should they choose you? What makes you different and valuable to them?	• Quality product • Quality Service • Value • Speed • Price point • Unique Process	• Experience • Proven results • Endorsed by a trusted 3rd party • Low risk • Rewards program for loyalty and referrals • Guarantees or warranties to instill confidence
WHY: What do they need that they can't or won't do for themselves that you can do well for them?	• Easy to execute and please • Appreciate you & your team • Most profitable • Repeat or referral business	• Cheapest to find • Large market, large demand • Makes you & your team feel great

CHAPTER SEVEN

Sales and Sales Management

Consider these head-turning statistics:

- "Sales jobs… are highly prized positions… but they can be extremely demanding, putting employees under inordinate pressure to cut corners."[39] – *The New York Times*, 2016.

- According to *Forbes*, almost 75% of sales people surveyed in a recent study said they have NOT received formal training from their company on how to use social media at all, while those who have been using it are quickly gaining a competitive advantage.[40]

- A 2016 *Harvard Business Review* study of sales professionals concluded, "while it's not surprising that top sales professionals are motivated by money—66% agreed with the statement out of 1,000 sales people and sales management leaders—they are also motivated by status and recognition. A staggering 84% indicated that being respected and recognized as one of the best by their peers at their company is very important to them."[41]

I've said this many times before, and I'll say it a few more times just to be sure you've heard me: sales are the life-blood of any organization, because without sales you have no revenue, and with no revenue you will soon have no company.

That was the problem as Zenman.

Keith Roberts of Zenman:

We had a good reputation in the marketplace, but we weren't leveraging it and marketing ourselves effectively. Sales was the biggest thing that was broken at our company. After our first all-day session, Chris pulled me aside

[39] https://www.nytimes.com/2016/08/11/business/international/abbott-india-suicide-inhuman-drug-sales-tactics.html
[40] https://www.forbes.com/sites/markfidelman/2013/05/19/study-78-of-salespeople-using-social-media-outsell-their-peers
[41] https://hbr.org/2016/06/a-portrait-of-the-overperforming-salesperson

and said, "this is going to sink the ship if you don't fix it. Let's schedule time to figure out how you're going to resolve this, because I can help fix it with you."

We had people who were not salespeople in the sales seats, so the people fielding the calls were turning away leads. Instead of saying, "Yeah, we can do that, anything's possible, time and money are the only limitations," they would say, "Uh, sounds like that would take a lot, which would cost a lot of money" or "Well, we haven't exactly done that before..." We had a salesperson who was trained as an attorney, not as a salesperson, and it was just torpedoing us.

I've found that my clients who have sales problems usually have a bunch of other problems within their businesses, too, which I like to refer to as "Third World" problems. And those clients who are doing well in sales often don't have an effective sales management process. They lose some of the sales they should be capturing, which results in lost business. A "First World" problem is more like, "where are we going to put the pool table and what color Ferrari should I drive to work today?"

So, at either end of the spectrum, whether you're in the First or Third world, you're going to have problems because sales are life. In this chapter, we'll look at what a Business Sergeant can do to build and strengthen the lifeblood of their organization.

LESSON 48 ★ Never Hire Your Best Salesperson to be Your Sales Manager

Sales are life. If you screw up that part of your business, you'll end up living in the Third World. To prevent that from happening, you need somebody to be accountable for the management of your salespeople.

But the first important lesson to always remember is this: NEVER hire your best salesperson to be your sales manager. That's because selling and managing sales people are two very different things, two super-different specialties. I've seen it over and over again in working with entrepreneurs and their sales teams—salespeople who LOVE selling usually HATE managing! The go-getter who makes the big sale is not typically the type of person who has the patience to supervise and train other salespeople.

I often see companies promoting their top salesperson to be the sales manager; the wheels soon come off and they wonder why. To make the distinction clear:

a sales manager is somebody who spends approximately a third of their time training salespeople (often in the field), a third of their time coaching and holding their salespeople accountable to the results of that training, and a third of their time recruiting new salespeople to replace the ones who can't meet the standard.

Here's another way to look at it: in sales, a third of the people are on their way in, excited and learning this new field; the third in the middle are your core producers, your war horses; and the other third are on their way out. So a sales manager's job is to

1. Make sure that high-quality people are in that first third.

2. Ensure the people in the middle third are getting everything they need in order to remain successful.

3. Rescue some of the people in the remaining third. If your sales manager can't do those three things well, then you need to find the right sales manager as quickly as possible.

New hires	Top producers	Re-train or re-home
Hire the best available	Support the top sellers	Save those you can; fire those you can't.

This issue was on full display in *Glengarry Glen Ross* between Kevin Spacey, the sales manager, and his sales team, which included high performers played to perfection by Al Pacino and Jack Lemon. Spacey was viewed as an office babysitter by the team (a lackey of Mitch and Murry, the owners of the real estate firm they all work for), not a fearless sales leader who was respected and revered.

A good sales manager must be able to do the sales job they are asking their team to perform, and be able and willing to coach others to success. That person should be someone who understands salespeople well and who understands exactly how to manage them. They shouldn't come from another part of the company; the sales team will in most cases only respect someone who can go out and do what they do.

Your potential sales manager might be someone on your existing sales team who, while not an over-performer, steadily hits their numbers each month, knows the job, but might be better suited to train other newcomers in the basics of the sales process. Or someone who's a little bit older and has a decades-rich resume of success as a sales producer. He or she might be ripe for a management position that doesn't require the same demands as being out in the field. These are the kinds of distinctions you need to make as a business owner when you're putting together your company's sales structure.

If you have a sales support person masquerading as a sales manager, your sales team will see through it every time. Your sales leader must be competent in her sales ability *and very talented* in her ability to lead others. If not, your sales team will treat the manager like a substitute teacher and shenanigans will likely ensue.

LESSON 49 ★ Take a Tough-Love Approach to Your Sales Team

One of the main points of this chapter is that if you don't have strong sales, you'll die as a small business. The second is: DON'T confuse sales and sales management. Equally as important to a Business Sergeant is learning how to manage the sales manager: your sales manager has got to be a bit of a Sergeant for sure, but (s)he also has to be managed correctly. NOT managing your Sales Manager is a very big problem. Sales is a hard job; there's a lot of rejection, a lot of getting outside your comfort zone, a lot of long, fast-paced days—it's kind of a crazy lifestyle. It can be very lucrative, so the juice is worth the squeeze, and that's why sales people are commonly the most highly paid people at the company. It's a very difficult and dynamic position, and few become true all-stars.

If you have a team of three or more people, you'll need a sales manager, but that person shouldn't have more than 10 to 12 people underneath them because it's really hard to lead larger teams, and you'll lose the right ratio of sales leader to sales followers for them to be as effective as possible, besides that's a lot of your company's fate to put in one person's hands. Being a salesperson is HARD; there's loads of rejection and, to be honest, not a lot of people can make it in sales. To recruit great salespeople onto your team, you'll need to reinforce everything we've talked about in terms of culture. Keep the bar high for the caliber of BOTH your salespeople and sales management. One can't exist without the other, which I learned first-hand in running my own team. It's a huge error to assume that because someone can outsell the rest of your team, that person will be just as successful at teaching everyone else to produce at that level. Sometimes it's the exact opposite. They're producing at that level because you've given giving them the freedom to go out on the front lines for you. But that's a different skill from being solely focused on managing the team back home.

Being a sales manager requires a tough-love kind of approach as a Business Sergeant, because your sales team is like the infantry in the army, and their weapons are your sales process and presentation. Sales people by definition are paid to manipulate other people to do what you want them to do, so don't be surprised if they try to manipulate you, their boss. That's why it's crucial in building and running a strong sales team to have a really strong sales manager who can maintain order and discipline to a sometimes "wild bunch". You're paying that person to prevent your salespeople from manipulating you and others in your business.

Another crucial lesson is to avoid cluttering your salespeople's calendars with non-sales activities. In the end, you need to hold them accountable for their sales numbers and you don't give them any excuses for why they weren't out there making sales. Keep your salespeople focused on what they do best. There are only so many people on the planet who are good at it; if you're fortunate to have those people, don't waste their time with non-sales B.S. If you do, you'll water down their effectiveness for your organization and you might just lose them. I know that's a little tough love from the Business Sergeant, but it's that important.

LESSON 50 ★ Always align Your Salespeople's Compensation

Salespeople's compensation should reflect how valuable they are to the company. Said another way, you want to compensate these people in a manner that provides your desired business results. A lot of times salespeople will sit on the bench because it doesn't make a big difference in their income to be hungry and land clients you didn't think you'd get. In those cases, I would literally double their commission if they got their own lead vs. depending on me to provide them leads. I've also seen commission plans that demotivated the team, or put your company's efforts at odds with their comp plan, these two need to be perfectly aligned! Salespeople will generally do what is in their best interest, so if you can align their AND your interests, you can avoid a lot of brain damage constantly fighting against the grain.

I had a lot of turnover while I built the team because it wasn't an hourly opportunity, but those people who liked working on commission and could perform made big money in just 4 or 5 hours a day. I want salespeople on my team who are hungry for uncapped opportunity.

It's important to energize your sales team, to get them fired up. Selling is a hard business. If you're not up for it, better that you do something else. Your sales team has to perform like a highly motivated military unit that is psyched up to charge into battle together. That mentality is crucial, and once you have an alignment of priorities, great execution will result.

LESSON 51 ★ Be Honest When Negotiating

Sales is a dance. What the client tells you isn't always what he wants, and based on whom you're dealing with, there's essentially a game of poker being player. There's an old sales saying: "Buyers are liars." I don't want to wholeheartedly agree with that statement, but sometimes both salespeople and buyers don't feel they have to be totally honest when haggling because it's part of the mindset of "negotiating."

In many cultures, it's acceptable to not tell the 100% truth when negotiating, whether people admit it or not, because salespeople do it to customers and vice versa. So, my philosophy is go out of your way to be upfront, open, and honest. It's refreshing. If you're brutally honest with people, they'll often say, "wow, I didn't expect this answer," and it endears you to them.

LESSON 52 ★ You Need a Repeatable System

You either have a systemized, repeatable sales system, or you're "winging it." As Matt Jaffe of 303 Software found out the hard way:

> One of our biggest problems was we didn't have any kind of sales operation. We were pretty much 100% reactive, so we were just fielding leads of various quality and referrals and turning those into new business. We had no sales operation, no sales program, we had nothing, and we decided that we would try to hire a sales executive who knew how to build a sales program. When we did, it turned out the guy was a really good salesman in terms of telling us what he could do for the company, but in executing he did nothing.

Your job as a Business Sergeant is to pick a sales system that works well for you and your business, and then develop a military mindset in executing that chosen methodology. This is one area within the business that requires a level of discipline and accountability above and beyond any other part of your company. Sales is a brutal and unforgiving profession; it requires a lot of tenacity, discipline, and accountability to get really good at it. So, it's super important to create a repeatable system for getting leads and closing them.

A systematized sales process asks and answers these questions:

- Once we've got that lead from marketing, what do we do with it?

- What things do our salespeople say? What do they do?

- What information do we provide to prospective clients?

- What questions do we ask to get prospective clients to a yes/no answer?

- How do we demonstrate our product or service to show value to prospective clients?

- How do we move the conversation to close the sale?

The sales management process is ensuring the sales people follow this system, because it's very easy in sales to get away from the system. In order to have great results, you need to manage your sales team and hold them accountable to the system you develop together with them.

As you're getting your sales team aligned to these guiding principles, the first order of business is to create an actual selling system: How are we going to take opportunities, how are we going to close them, and what is our best foot forward toward that goal? If your business doesn't have a system, the first thing you're going to want to do is some A/B testing until you find a system that fits your company. And, most importantly, one that produces measurable results when you put that system into action. Once you have that system, the next step is to get your staff to follow it religiously so everyone can enjoy more consistent results and identify and pinpoint opportunities for improvement.

Some important steps toward creating a successful sales process involve knowing:

- What is the message?

- Where are the differentiators?

- What are the tools you're going to give the salespeople?

- How are our sales people are going to be judged?

Equally important is creating a seamless transition from branding to marketing to your sales process. Your brand is what people say when you're not around. Branding means creating an aura around your product and services—your color palette, your logo, your reputation, your messaging; everything that goes into your brand. The marketing is about how you deploy that brand to your ideal clients so you're not sending that message to people who won't do business with you (otherwise known as wasting a ton of money). So, you need to shine a spotlight directly on the area of your market your business serves. Then use your marketing to translate the brand so it enhances the consumer's perception of you and makes your solution to their problem more attractive, and ultimately they take action with you.

So for instance, you wouldn't want to be promoting an upscale brand and come out with 99-cent coupons. Then, to take it one step further, when a client begins the sales experience at your company, that experience must be congruent with your marketing and branding. If all those aspects don't match, you're confusing your customer with conflicting messaging.

The process the sales manager creates for their salespeople should be natural, conversational, steeped in logic, and be a no-brainer. The best sales presentation is one that makes it easy to do business with you, where you're pleasant and helpful. When a customer feels they've made a great decision, and your product or service does exactly what it's supposed to do, you have a solid track record (referrals and testimonials) that you can use to attract more customers. Simple, right?

For instance, after a couple of years working with a dozen or so leadership teams in Denver, my phone started to ring. Before that, nobody knew what my personal brand was or what I could do for them. Now, people will come up to me and say, "Oh yeah, I've heard of you—you combine a military mindset with the entrepreneurial operating system to get great results! I hear people are really getting things done with your Hoo-Rah approach!"

I've seen it happen many times and it's important to understand that dynamic. Your results and what people say about you are more important than the sale, because if you and your company are concentrating on "delivering the goods" the selling becomes so much easier. Consumers are smart; they know when you're phoning it in as a company or as a salesperson. So, remember if you do great things at a competitive market rate, you'll always stay busy.

In getting to these goals, it's important to first understand what your company's system is: what you do and why. With every "fresh" inbound lead, if the marketing's basically already done, then what is the sales process moving forward? How do your people contact the lead? What's their opener on the call? You should always have a greeting already worked out, your pitch, and the resonating message that will keep the prospective buyer on the line longer than your first few words.

So, for instance, an opening line that always worked well for my employees when I was running a sales team was to say, "Good morning, Mr/Mrs._____, I'm responding to your request. I would love to talk to you about how we can help. Do you have five minutes to talk?" Every little detail has to be put into a process and outlined, and it has to be executed the same way across your entire sales team. Now, obviously, each sales person has his or her own individual style and personality that influences their approach, but your sales management team will have refined and tested and honed that presentation until it's razor sharp.

By then, no matter who's occupying one of your sales seats, your sales managers can plug them right in and say, "follow this system because we know it works." The more direction your sales people have, the more it will help them maximize their time, which is crucial when contacting potential leads. By maximizing their time, they will be making that many more quality sales calls a day. So, when you've A/B tested that system (just as you tested your marketing process) and once you've produced your best results on a consistent basis, there's no reason to constantly try to tinker with it and improve it past an acceptable point. My advice is: Once it's as good as you think it's going to get (you're exceeding industry standards, margins are great etc.), stop trying to tweak things. Let that system run and focus on other parts of your business that need the same kind of attention. Remember: good things always happen when a good process is repeated. The numbers will speak volumes.

LESSON 53 ★ Teach Your Sales Team to Close at a Higher Rate

As a business owner figuring out where to spend your money, it's key to remember that marketing opportunities are expensive. You'll need to figure out what's your maximum acceptable marketing spend and stick to it. How much additional business can your system handle? What is the most amount of business you've been able to do in a single month (your maximum capacity)? I like to take 10% to 20% off that, and you should be able to do that on a regular basis without overstretching your team.

To determine that number, look at the historical data. But if you have one salesperson selling 10 units a week and the rest of your people selling 3 a week, is it because the 10-unit salesperson is superhuman, or because the 3-unit people need some enhanced training? Sometimes there's a very small distance in ability and training between the people selling 10 units a week and those selling only 3.

Let me use a baseball analogy to explain this. If you're hitting .245, you're in the minor leagues making 60K a year, slogging around the country on a bus, and sleeping two to a room with your teammates in cheap motels. But if you improve that to .275, you might find yourself in the major leagues making $5M a year and sleeping in a room of your own at the Waldorf Astoria. Take this to the next level—hit just a few more balls and slug .355, and you'll be an All-Star making $20M a year, with your very own jet and lots of great endorsement deals.

Note that the difference between an All-Star and a minor leaguer is just a few more hits. It's the same in sales. There's a very small difference between the best and the rest. The best sales people, the ones who really want "it," have that same competitive, go-getter, get better personality as All-Star players do.

That's what every sales manager and business owner needs to understand: If you can train and motivate your people to raise their sales closing percentage from 20% to 35%, they can move from the minor leagues to the majors. In the process, you can almost double your revenue without spending another dollar. Your fixed costs stay the same and incremental income comes in at a nice profit. Leading your sales team to close at a higher rate is one of the easiest ways to simply make more money for your company.

On the flipside, if you're not getting the sales and your competitors are soundly beating you, if your company's getting smaller while your competitors grow larger and move ahead at an accelerated rate, you will eventually get "squeezed" out of business. You can't get sales wrong because you'll run out of time and money before you have a chance to recover. Once you burn through your cash and have no new opportunities to sell, you're a business casualty.

That's why it makes sense to hit a bigger number for a while before you add fixed cost resources to support those sales, because if your sales level recedes back to the old number, you'll be running at a lower margin covering those increased costs without the sales to support them.

LESSON 54 ★ Always be Aware of the Costs of Your Sales Organization

What I've seen and learned time and time again in business is this: Always fully understand what your costs are. For instance, a lot of entrepreneurs say, "aaah, salespeople normally make 10%." And my routine response is: "Yeah, but they also make 1.2 times that base amount with social security, FICA, and there are always additional costs for meals and entertainment, etc."

So any time you're trying to figure your costs, make sure you understand the concept of "fully loaded costs", i.e., benefits, tax burden, compliance-related costs, training and related allowances, parking/travel, lodging, computers, smartphones, etc.—anything you need to spend out of pocket to get them started. When you hire a new salesperson, you're not just hiring that person; you're also hiring new equipment, sales samples and new marketing materials. As a small business owner, you really have to understand the fully loaded costs inside your sales organization.

LESSON 55 ★ Train Your Salespeople

It's crucial to make sure your salespeople know how to both open the door to a sale and then CLOSE the sale once interest arises. I've witnessed potential deals fall apart right as they were about to happen because the salesperson wasn't properly trained by their team leaders on how to cover both ends of the process. While your sales people need to be given a certain amount of latitude and freedom to close sales, they also need very clear and easy-to-use, *in-the-heat-of-the-moment pricing guidelines*. When a potential client starts to express interest, and seems in the mood to do a deal right there, your salespeople need to be nimble enough to not lose that "let's do a deal right now" mentality because that opportunity might never return. At that point, your salesperson has only opened the door to the possibility of doing a deal. They must know how to close the door as well.

This is the most crucial and yet most easily fumbled part of closing the deal. They need to be able to close with confidence. The greatest help sales management can provide is to not saddle your salespeople with algorithms so complex that they can't figure things out on the fly. Once that momentum is stalled, the prospective client will sense it and often back out because it no longer "feels right."

When I first start coaching businesses on sales improvement many years ago, I found that less than half the clients I met really understood the sales process, and fewer have a very consistent sales pipeline vs. a lumpy or sporadic pipeline. As we worked together, sales start to grow consistently each quarter, sometimes by a little and sometimes by a LOT, and the clients now know WHY they're successful. Equally as important, they can literally turn the marketing wick up or down (depending on when their sales momentum dictates it), and the sales they close are in direct correlation to those marketing adjustments they make.

Probably 60% of the companies I work with, at the outset of our collaboration, don't have a consistent and repeatable sales process. If they have a spike in sales, it's short-lived because they don't have a process to understand how they did it and that can repeat the success. They often chalk it up to luck, but as the famous saying goes, "90% of sales is process, 10% is good old-fashioned luck." Your sales process should be custom-manufactured. When you don't have one in play, it creates pain all around in the company. It can become an uncomfortable place to work, especially if you're part of the sales team. The entire company is relying on that team to generate the income that supports the business, and they therefore deserve not only the support of the rest of the company, but also a reliable process that generates leads and closes them at a high percentage.

LESSON 56 ★ Create Incentives for Your Salespeople

Your salespeople have to be appropriately paid for what they do. In some organizations, the sales process is severely compartmentalized, either because it's complex or easier to scale, or it's better to have a subject matter expert for conversion rates. Whatever the reason, their people are usually paid a smaller amount because they're a part of the cog. Better to pay your salespeople and your sales manager in ways that benefit the sales people and the company. That isn't always the case. A lot of times we'll develop a top plan that will incentivize certain behaviors that aren't necessarily what we want as a company. If we want salespeople to be making calls, outside of the leads we provide them as an organization, then we should pay them more money. Why not encourage them while they're out doing that, so at least when they get it done they know they're in bonus land? It makes that extra work they had to endure worth it, and they're more likely to do it again because the measure of their effort is reflected in their paycheck.

If your commission plans don't align with what the company wants, it can create selfish salespeople. There are several warnings signs to watch out for. I've seen bonus plans designed to get a sale in a given sales period *or* in the next month where they know they have more traction. As a consequence, they're either delaying or hurrying a customer. So as a sales manager, you want to make sure that sales contests have incentives outside of the regular commission to keep things fun, interesting, and fair. You want to make sure that what's good for the company is good for the sales rep, vs. what's good for the sales rep is good for the sales rep, and not the company. I hammer home this point because you need to make sure that your incentives are in line with your goals and your culture.

With my background in the military, I've always been attracted to using uniforms and insignia, and have always tried use similar incentives with my sales teams that weren't just financial. So, for instance, you can create the President's Club for the elite performers on your sales and marketing teams, or the concept of varsity vs. junior varsity teams, i.e., your A and B sales teams. It's about letting your A players feel a sense of accomplishment while motivating your JV team, who will work that much harder to put points on the board and make it onto the A team's roster.

As the sales manager, or coach in this metaphor, it's your job to create a ladder or path forward for those JV players. And unlike the military, where every promotion is based on a classification, in the business world it's about figuring out how you give someone rank. The harder they play, the higher up they go, and the more money and distinction they earn. Designing this kind of achievable track that ignites upward momentum is key to creating a successful and highly productive sales team. I recommend creating a career progression level that you can militarize or incentivize to further motivate your staff.

Always remember that salespeople by nature are big personalities and very competitive; if you don't find something for them to latch onto, they will float away like balloons. You want to keep them grounded but also challenged by constantly training them and helping them evolve in their craft, and by providing them with very clear boxes to check off when successful.

First we create that mindset, then we create the environment, then we create a system, and then we have to hold them accountable in military-style fashion. The neat thing about the military's approach is that when you do something really cool, you are recognized in front of your peers. By the same token, if you screw up everybody's doing to know about it. You can do the same: reward high performance and at the same time put everyone's numbers up on the board week in and out; the team should know when one of their members isn't performing as well.

Create a bunch of incentives: contests, free tickets to sports or cultural events, trips to Vegas (always a big hit with sales people). When I was running my own sales team, we had lobsters and bacon-wrapped fillets on the grill for lunch when we had strong sales weeks, and peanut butter and jelly on Wonder bread when we had low sales weeks. My sales people always knew week in and out how they were performing.

If your business is manufacturing, find ways to motivate the machine operators and gamify what can be a very repetitive workplace. Put a big scoreboard on the wall that shows production numbers by each shift. Create a competition between work groups to gain more commitment and create personal fulfillment and satisfaction. When you create contests, the competitive juices start flowing. That's what I learned in the military. The incentive is not about money—it's about being number one.

In the military, the winners get a 3-day pass. The losers have to sweep the parking lot while wearing pink tutus (or something like that). The losers have to do something a little embarrassing, which leads to picture taking and pointing and laughing. That's what makes winning so great and losing so bad. Create a competition where everyone's ready to give it their best because they either enjoy being the winners or they hate being the losers. Either way, it's motivational and fun. Again, you're not trying to motivate people from 0 to 100; you're getting people who are already at 70 to move up 10, 20, or 30 points.

LESSON 57 ★ Trade the "Brilliant Jerk" to Another Team

You also need to watch out for hotshots on your sales team (and in other parts of your organization) who display what is commonly referred to as "The Brilliant Jerk Syndrome." This is someone who sold a million units last year but is a prima donna who doesn't want to follow process or attend sales meetings with everyone else. This person is not a team player, even if they put big points on the board. If you let "stars" like this run roughshod over the rules, they'll come to believe that they're untouchable because they make it rain so hard. Even superstar athletes like Michael Jordan and Wayne Gretzky needed to be team players; they listened to their coaches and followed the plays that were called.

If you want to build a great culture on your sales team, there's no reason to accept that kind of behavior. You can still acknowledge that A player as a V.I.P. with the enhanced incentives we discussed above, but everyone on your sales staff should be expected to follow the same process. That will prevent resentment in the ranks and will encourage healthy competition to put the big points on the board.

NBA coach Phil Jackson spoke to the importance of this sense of fair play when he said, "Good teams become great ones when the members trust each other enough to surrender the Me for the We. The sign of a great player is how much he elevates his colleagues' performance."

If you encourage this kind of culture, your team is far more likely to make it into the sales playoffs; if you don't encourage it, you're ultimately holding them back while only the Brilliant Jerk gets ahead. And believe me, he's playing for himself, not the team. So, while it might look like a bad move to trade a Brilliant Jerk to another team, it's actually a smart play for the team's greater good. Once the Brilliant Jerk is removed from the team, everyone will see you're really serious about creating and protecting a great culture for everyone to enjoy together.

LESSON 58 ★ Have a Plan to Improve Your Sales Team

If you have sales members on your team who are not performing, what's the plan to get them to perform? After-action reviews are important here, as well as listening in on some of their sales calls to find out how you can help them improve. It's also important to ask a lot of questions, to do a lot of triage and diagnostic work to find out where that sales person is failing. They might be doing 9 steps flawlessly out of your 10-step sales process, but if they're getting that one key step wrong, the sale isn't going to happen. Great sales management has to put a great training and coaching program in place, because there are very few salespeople who are born sellers that don't require any direction. Even someone with the greatest natural sales instinct had to hone that talent along the way, usually with the help of a mentor who showed that person the ropes.

Forecasting your sales accurately is another important issue to pay attention to. You can't just make up a figure every day; you need metrics to measure the baseline, even though your salespeople have to be given a little bit of latitude. Whatever the learning curve may be for your industry, you have to give your people the time and attention to get them there when they're first starting out. But once you've established a given baseline for a salesperson and they're not excelling beyond that latitude, you need to start firing people to make room for those who can do the job. The trick is, you don't want to do this too early; they might not have gotten all the training they need or enough time in the field to learn the route/customer base. It's very important to remember that salespeople just starting out can get wrapped around the axle. So the last thing you want to do is fire people who might have the potential to stay in that middle third.

That said, way too many small business owners hang on to dead weight for way too long. When I work with new clients and start digging into their staff issues, I routinely find salespeople who haven't met their quotes (sometimes for years) and are still around. It just blows me away when a company is still employing someone who hasn't made the numbers three quarters in a row. It's important to never overpromise anything upfront and to set realistic vs. unrealistic expectations for your sales team.

So, it's very important to create an eco-system that will enable you to recognize underperformance in sales and the steps needed to improve it. Without that, your company won't survive. The sales manager has to keep their finger on the pulse of the team's daily lead flow and go on sales calls because, as we say in the military, you can't lead your troops from battalion headquarters. You have to be out on the business battlefield with your troops.

FOCUS ON THE CLIENT
Defining the Sales Pipeline at LPR Construction

Not many businesses are nearly full for the year they're in, let alone half-way to the next year. But such is the case with LPR Construction, a $100M per year structural steel and industrial contractor.

The company never had a sales problem. What they needed help with was managing the sales process. They weren't happy about the margins on a couple of very large jobs that didn't look great, and my advice was to pass on the stuff they weren't excited about to leave room for the stuff that did excite them.

Let's hear Linc Turner, the company's president, tell the story:

> We were in a transitional period where we had some people who were retiring and had a younger generation who were coming up into more leadership roles, and we were also in a transitional point in the organization where we were going from just our typical organic growth to starting to expand and looking to do some acquisitions to increase our growth and profitability.

> We were definitely looking at different ways of organizing the company and increasing accountability and expectations. I was referred to Chris and he presented to my YPO (Young Presidents Organization) Forum on a Friday. I had an executive team meeting on Monday, and I re-organized our agenda and brought him back that day to talk to us again. On our very first day with him we reorganized our executive management team and eliminated an executive position. Within a month, we already implemented additional organizational changes.

> We've always had a very strong sales organization, but we've better defined the customers that we want to really focus on, where we're going to spend our time and our efforts. We're about 95% sold out for this year and I already have a backlog of 50% for next year. We have enough revenue sold for next year that we've pretty much covered all of our overhead for that year.

> We have reorganized our leadership team and better defined our roles, and as a result the whole team is working better together.

A Brief History of After Action Reviews (AARs)

The "After Action Review" was first developed as a learning methodology in the 1970s by the U.S. Army. Its purpose was to create a structured means to facilitate day-to-day learning from combat training exercises. The reasons for success or failure in combat training exercises are often not clear. AARs were designed to tease out the lessons learned from such exercises.

The AAR methodology has been extremely successful in the U.S. Army and today is so firmly embedded in its culture that an AAR takes place after every training event and they are also used after military actions or operations. When I served, after every training event, and after every operation, we would usually be tired, hungry, sore and ready to hit the rack, (or the bar!) but we all knew we had one thing left to do: go to the AAR and extract all the lessons we learned, so we could be better for the next round of training or operations. I like to say, "you win or you learn." In other words, you're never "losing" if you do it right.

AARs were first adopted in business in the late '90s. I have used AARs in my business career to make sure that I, or someone who I manage, gets the biggest bang for both the sales calls that worked, and the ones that didn't. After all, if it works, wouldn't we want to know why so we could do it again? And conversely if it didn't, we should probably look at what we are doing and change it for future sales calls.

Key takeaways for conducting an AAR

- They always go better if you have multiple perspectives. If you're only using one perspective, it will be hard to see the other side… Because there is only one!

- Have them as soon as you can after the event, you'll lose valuable data and the "feel" of how things went if you wait too long.

- Create an open and honest environment. If your sales rep knows they will get the stick if they "confess" they simply won't, and everyone will miss that opportunity for improvement.

- The results of your AAR should lead to new or refresher training on whatever insights we gained from it. Customize your training, so your rep can see themselves winning in the future with their new knowledge or proficiency.

- Record and document the AAR's outcomes and insights, so you can track any patters or trends with your sales people. This will help your rep to commit to corrective action, and it will help your sales manager focus on the right training and accountability actions with that rep.

- Celebrate and socialize the results of a successful sales call following corrective training, so the true value of the AAR will be known. This will show the immense value to your sales reps, and make them more inclined to want to share, learn and grow in future AARs.

 ## AFTER-ACTION REVIEW (AAR) WITH NEXT STEPS

An AAR is an incredibly simple but powerful tool that allows individuals and teams to continuously learn from their everyday experiences. At the end of every event, a few simple questions are asked:

1. What were the desired outcomes? _____

_____

_____

_____

2. What were the actual outcomes? _____

_____

_____

_____

3. Why were the outcomes different to those planned? _____

_____

_____

_____

_____

4. What was learned? _____

_____

_____

_____

_____

CLIENT EXAMPLE OF SALES PROCESS (FROM LEAD TO CLOSE)

Pilots, regardless of their experience level, complete a pre-flight checklist every time they get on a plane. The pre-flight checklist helps to ensure that no critical step is overlooked or forgotten even if the pilot is in a hurry or preoccupied with other issues. In the same way, a sales process checklist can help you to track each stage of the sales cycle and is the first step to creating a sales process plan.

The specific form of your sales process will vary depending on the nature of your products and the type of prospect you sell to. A salesperson selling expensive manufacturing equipment to large companies will have a much longer and more complicated process than a salesperson selling used books door-to-door to consumers. However, any salesperson, regardless of product type, can benefit from a checklist review. Here is an example of a simple sales process checklist that might suit your needs.

Basic Sales Process

Prospecting for Leads

- ☐ Lead list checked against database for duplicate
- ☐ Lead fits basic prospect requirements (e.g. income level, type of business, etc.)

Setting Appointment

- ☐ Initial contact made (phone call, email, in-person visit, etc.)
- ☐ Pre-qualification completed
- ☐ Appointment scheduled
- ☐ Researched prospect to determine needs

Presentation

- ☐ Final qualification completed – prospect is a true opportunity
- ☐ Prospect needs assessed
- ☐ Decision maker identified
- ☐ Purchasing process and requirements identified
- ☐ Next steps determined (scheduled a second meeting, collected RFP requirements, etc.)

Closing

- ☐ Prospect objections & questions addressed
- ☐ Appropriate product/service type selected and accepted
- ☐ Customer signed contract
- ☐ Asked customer for permission to use as a reference or testimonial
- ☐ Asked customer for referrals

Post-Closing

- ☐ Reported sale to sales manager
- ☐ Order processed and filled
- ☐ Sent thank-you note to customer
- ☐ Followed up to confirm customer satisfaction
- ☐ Resolved any questions or problems

Credit to Wendy Connick

CHAPTER EIGHT

Know Your Numbers!

Bill Gates, Microsoft Founder and longtime CEO, once said, "knowing your numbers is a fundamental precept of business." This is a business basic echoed over and over by the world's leading entrepreneurial success stories, from Fortune 500 companies on down to the everyday small-business owner.

The Business Journal adds this advice: "Numbers tell the unvarnished truth about how a business is doing… The key for the entrepreneur is to know what numbers are the bellwethers for their business. Track them, stay tuned to what impacts them, and continually strive to make them stronger."[43]

Yet, believe or not, many entrepreneurs find it hard to focus on the numbers. I see this a lot—business owners who don't really know the financials and just operate on gut feeling. Consider American Express's acknowledgment that, "as a small-business owner, your days are packed with an endless number of tasks that keep your business on track. When you do finally flop down exhausted on the couch after work, it's probably not to pour over your financial statements."[44]

When your books don't square, that can be a dangerously ignorant way to do business. As a consequence, you can wake up one day to a nightmare scenario that is completely avoidable. All you need are some basic proactive steps on your part to ensure you have the mechanisms in place to keep regular track of your numbers. *Inc.* magazine reminds us, "business owners have a tendency to rely heavily on their accountants when it comes to tracking their company's critical numbers. Having a strong relationship with a reliable CPA is certainly a must for any business, but you can never forget as a business owner that responsibility for the financial health of your company rests ultimately with you and you alone."[45]

SO PAY ATTENTION!

[43] http://www.bizjournals.com/bizjournals/how-to/growth-strategies/2015/03/business-owners-need-to-know-these-4-things.html

[44] https://www.americanexpress.com/us/small-business/openforum/articles/the-7-financial-numbers-every-business-owner-should-know

[45] https://www.inc.com/guides/tracking-critical-numbers.html

I can tell you another thing—if you don't know your numbers, then you're sitting on what I like to call the Chaos Meter, which in business is ALWAYS ticking! If a business is at zero on the Chaos Meter, they have a system in place for everything, and they've automated it with technology or a solid process that is consistently followed by everyone. In contrast, if you go up to a 10 on the meter, it means (literally) that there's a wad of cash in a desk drawer, people stick their hands in there, grab some, and then run out the door with little to no accountability or any accounting system of where the money is going.

Most companies probably rank at 4 or a 5 on the Chaos Meter. They're able to function. But until you install financial controls, systems, policies, and procedures, the chaos never completely goes away. Until then, your business will stay in a kind of a free-for-all, where there's a lot of gray area and a lot of those mistakes will be made. And these mistakes can be *very* costly.

Think of your cash flow in the context of your sales or production pipeline—if your pipeline is lumpy, it's really hard to run the business. That's why you need to have a core process down pat—a really good brand, great marketing, strong sales management, a great sales closing, and client onboarding and fulfillment operations. When you have all those things, your business will be a more consistent, scalable organization. If you're a $12 million company, and one month you're at $978,000 and the next month you're at $1,000,051, that's pretty consistent. But if one month you're at $600,000 and the next it's $1.2 million, that's a start-stop/rubber band situation. Either you're burning labor with people on your payroll who aren't being utilized, or you're understaffed. But when you have a consistent pipeline and operation, it's because you know your numbers and have the metrics to measure them professionally and consistently.

LESSON 59 ★ Have a Budget

The first number you need to know better than any other is your budget. Having one in place is crucial and the bottom line is this: you either have a plan or you don't. It's amazing how many companies I work with—and I'm talking about $5, $10, $20 million businesses—*that have never had a formal budget!*

These businesses don't really understand why they're successful. They might have a vague idea, but it's not until I urge them to create a budget that they have any clear idea of what they're doing. I'll get comments like: "Holy crap, I had no idea all these little things added up to such a big thing at the end of the year!"

Every business is different financially; some have really great cash flow by design, and some have really poor cash flow where one mistake or delay can put them at a deficit financially, either on a project or overall basis. While it's very important to have a budget, it's even more important that someone is actually enforcing it. Is someone overspending? Underspending? What happens when we are off target?

If you're a successful business generating $17 million a year in revenue but you have less than 5% net profit and never had a formal budget, that might be the reason why. You may have plenty of top-line revenue and a lot of people who want to do business with your company, but you need to have controls in place to avoid crappy financial visibility. Bringing in financial efficiency experts like part-time controllers or a fractional CFO is a really easy way to help get this process started. In fact, I work with a company right now whose express purpose is to go into businesses and do just that.

This is the one area where there are a lot of outside resources available, especially if you're a small business operating under $1 to $5 million in sales. I see a lot of lack of sophistication in this area. Remember, there are no points for second place in business, and this is one area where even if you think you understand it, you still need to have a specialist who really gets it help you develop a plan and a budget. Someone who can help build in mechanisms to reward people for finding cost savings.

For instance, when I was a small business owner, if you could save me money, I'd give you 10% of the savings as a commission for the first 90 days. One employee at my construction company found me a dumpster company that led to me saving quite a bit of money, like $2,000 a month, so that that young man got a bonus of $200 X 3= $600 total! If you are paying a 10% commission on the savings for a quarter, keep in mind that I was still keeping 90% of the savings, so it was a great deal for everybody. So be creative in finding ways to save. It's not what you make in business, it's what you keep, and not understanding that can cost you a lot of money, a lot of missed opportunities, and quite possibly your business itself. As the business sergeant, I'm going to give you a little bit of tough love here: "If you don't know your numbers, you don't know jack!"

The funny thing about money is that banks always want to lend it to you when you don't need it, but when you desperately need it they're not usually going to lend it to you, or only at some ridiculous interest rate. If you don't understand your numbers very clearly and are even a little bit asleep at the wheel, the next thing you know, you'll be having trouble hitting your payroll on time, which is one of the *worst* things you can do as a business owner. When I see clients get into these types of spots, they usually have no idea what's going on or how or why they got there. They certainly can't give me the answer. Then we get a financial professional in there to do some forensic accounting and really dig to find the reason for the bleeding.

The business didn't have the parameters or the visibility with the numbers to know what was happening. They were operating from a position of absolute ignorance, and then they made a foolish financial decision like buying real estate or equipment, thinking they could afford it. So it's critical not to operate in a fog. Fox Business hammered home the point that, "when you own a small business, it is imperative that you keep a good set of books that are consistently and contemporaneously updated."[46] This allows you to know what moves you can and can't afford to make, and then you can plan strategically for when it's the best time to make them.

LESSON 60 ★ Understand Fully Loaded Costs

Along with keeping track of your budget, it's equally critical for you as an owner to fully understand the cost structures around your business, especially the concept of fully loaded costs.

I'll ask one of my clients what they're paying an employee, and when they give me a number like $50K, my response is: "Oh really? How many other costs did you incur to recruit them, hire them, train them, and pay them benefits on an ongoing basis?" There's this concept called "burden," and just the tax burden on an employee is usually putting 12% to 15% on top of whatever the tangibles and benefits are before even factoring the other fully loaded costs. So when I end up digging into that question a little bit, it usually turns out that the cost of an employee is not $50k but more like $57,500 ($50k x 1.15) PLUS whatever additional costs directly related to that employee, so that $50K can be well over 60K pretty quickly. It's crucial to understand fully loaded costs so you can get a true picture of your overhead.

If you can keep your costs within the guidelines of a healthy business, you're going to end the year a higher net profit, depending on how you do it. If you can't wrap your head around that as an entrepreneur, if you're just floating along in a fog about costs and figuring you must be doing alright if you have a little money left over at the end of the year… WRONG! That kind of winging-it approach is deadly in the military and business alike. The Huffington Post makes the reassuring point that, "knowing your numbers in your business doesn't need to be intimidating,"[47] especially if you bring in a specialist like a full- or part-time bookkeeper to help you get your house in order.

LESSON 61 ★ Hire a CFO or Other Financial Professional

There are a million ways to tweak and operate and maximize, but if you really don't understand what the averages are and whether you're operating below or above them, then it's really difficult to run your business successfully in the long run. Again, the best advice I could offer here is the need to utilize a CFO or other high-level financial professional to pin down the exact percentages for your industry. Hiring a part-time one is common in a small business operation. Best-selling business writer Dave Ramsey, author of *The Total Money Making Package*, endorsed this approach with his point that, "you *don't* have to hire a full-time bookkeeper or accountant to *keep* your finances organized."[48] This is where you or your support staff can keep the general ledger using off-the-shelf software, then have the pro check your work. This is an area where it pays to have another set of eyeballs on your books.

I'm a HUGE believer that if you don't have the budget to hire full-time seats to help you keep track of all of the aforementioned, or if you just don't have the need for a full-time bookkeeper, hire a fractional or part-time one who also works for some other business owners you know. In other words, a proven commodity, someone who comes highly recommended. This is very important because trying out a new finance person can be a scary thing. You can't afford a bad hire in this seat, and this is one position that is really difficult to unwind if you need to fire them. LinkedIn notes that although, "the term *'fractional employment'* has been around for several years, it is emerging as the new model for employment—especially in small and medium-sized businesses."[49]

This is a smart way to lessen your exposure in that key seat.

A CFO can help you establish important baselines for your business. You don't want to cut your marketing down to half a percent when it needs to be at 3, or else you'll eventually go out of business. You have to make sure you're watering the garden in the right places, and, equally as important, that you're not over-watering or under-watering.

[48] https://www.daveramsey.com/blog/focus-on-taxes-or-business-growth
[49] https://www.linkedin.com/pulse/fractional-employment-new-model-ron-jamieson
[47] http://www.huffingtonpost.com/craig-ballantyne/7-things-you-need-to-know_b_11391770.html

It's crucial against that backdrop to make sure you've set up some controls and safeties and checks and balances, so you're always spot-checking with your finance person, "hey, how are we doing?" In financial planning, we should know we need to save some money for the next couple quarters if we have a quarterly tax payment or a quarterly insurance payment coming up, because no matter what your fixed vs. fluctuating costs are, those expenses will always be there. You always need to have a plan and know what you're doing, and when an indicator says X, make sure you execute accordingly.

Forbes underscores this by reminding us, "at surface level, the primary reason businesses fail is they simply run out of cash."[50] So keeping track of your cash—from flow to reserves—is crucial, and to that end I recommend working with a finance professional at least once a quarter (assuming you don't have your own in-house) to stay on track. Be prepared to make changes quickly if they discover something that looks off.

Not everyone can be a Chief Financial Officer or a Comptroller or a C.P.A. That seat requires a specific skill set, just like sales or any other division in your operation. Make sure you hire someone who is wired that way, who's in love with numbers, because you want them to care that much about yours. Having a lazy accountant or C.P.A. running your company can be deadly. I've seen it all too often, where that huge responsibility for oversight is given to a family member or friend, someone who has no business managing that part of your business. Not all businesses need a high-level CFO on a regular basis; smaller ones can do fine with a controller or a bookkeeper with some high-level strategic oversight from a CFO annually or quarterly.

No visionary entrepreneur I know LOVES the nerdy side of numbers. It's a pain in the ass, and if you treat it like it's a pain in the ass, as most people do, and give it only minimal water and sunlight, it can be the very thing that brings the whole house crashing down. To protect against that, you must open your eyes and remember to take some basic preventive steps when filling this all-important seat. Be aware of what the healthy numbers are for your industry, and then find somebody who specializes in your industry, especially when it comes to complexities you don't fully understand. This is where you cannot afford to be cheap. It's just too important. So get a referral and interview a number of people before making a final decision, but don't scrimp on financial controls is my big message here. It will cost you dearly in the long run if you don't know your numbers.

---

[50] https://www.forbes.com/sites/ericwagner/2013/09/12/five-reasons-8-out-of-10-businesses-fail

If you've got really good financials, including 13-week cash flow projections, depreciation and amortization schedules, capital equipment expenses—all the basics a great numbers pro will know—then you're on the right track. But when someone says they need to make a substantial decision for the business, then it's time to bring in a specialist to get their expert opinion before making that big decision.

LESSON 62 ★ Have a Cash Reserve on Hand

In the military, we use the term "cache," which usually refers to a big pile of weapons and ammunition. In business it's called *cash,* and you should have at least 90 days of operating capital in the bank, ready to go for your current monthly burn rate.

Entrepreneur magazine warns, "no matter how many safeguards you have in place to protect your company's cash, hiccups in cash flow are a business reality. This may be no big deal if you have a cushion of savings on hand. But if your company is working from a zero account balance, one slow sales month could mean instant disaster."[51]

Everyone's going to sleep a little better when you have that cushion. If something bad happens, most businesses can usually rebound in a 90-day timeframe IF they have that much in reserves on hand. But if you only have two weeks of cash on hand and you need three weeks to fix a problem and return to normal operations, your company is out of business in that scenario. When you have reserves on hand, you prevent a mere flesh wound from becoming something fatal.

LESSON 63 ★ Have Controls in Place

Knowing your numbers as a business owner means you understand—and have controls in place for—the key factors that determine your profitability, and that you're equally able to pivot to save some profit when possible. Obviously, every business is different, but most businesses are looking at their sales price, their gross profit margin, and their costs of goods sold (COGS). Once you have all your expenses and know your above-the-line, which includes variable costs, material or labor costs, etc., or below-the-line, which are fixed costs like rent, electricity, etc., what you have left is your **net profit**.

So, for example, if you're starting off with a really strong gross profit margin like 50% to 70%, it's a little easier to execute, but if you've got weaker margins,

[51] https://www.entrepreneur.com/article/249020

like 15% to 25%, and your sales cost goes up 5% or 6%, you only have a 15% gross margin. You lost a ton of margin with a fluctuation of just 5 points. So it's critical to understand your key performance indicators so you can track how you're going to end up.

Here's an example of how a financial professional would model basic benchmarks for a software company to end the year with a 15% net profit.

Revenue	*100%*
COGS (Cost of goods sold)	
Full time Employees	*45%*
Contractors	*10%*
Gross Margin	*45%*
Operating Expenses	
G&A Salaries (General and Administrative)	*12.5%*
Sales	*6.0%*
Marketing	*2.0%*
Education/Training	*1.5%*
Recruiting	*1.0%*
IT (Information technology)	*2.0%*
Legal	*0.5%*
Non-Billable Travel	*1.0%*
Other (Miscellaneous Expenses)	*3.5%*
Total Operating Expenses	**30%**
EBITDA (Earnings before Interest, Taxes, Depreciation, and Amortization)	**15%**

LESSON 64 ★ Look at Historical Data

The above example is just a simple guideline for a software company. Meet with a finance pro who really understands your industry; run your numbers and see how many percentage points, plus or minus, you are under or over. Also, consider looking at your historical financial data. You might be able to spot trends and patterns that will help you steer your company to strong levels of profitability. Try to be within 0.5% of each one of these, and anything you have that is over 2% over or under you should really look at that. Look for any outliers and attack the one that's the most out of spec first. Then go down the line and continue to tweak until you fall into those suggested standards.

If you're able to get your company to do that, you'll be in a much better place to make a consistent profit at the end of each year.

LESSON 65 ★ Trust But Verify

Make sure you have an outside accountant conduct an audit. Sadly, I've seen a few painful instances where companies suffer from embezzlement of funds, usually in the finance departments of small, privately held companies (bookkeepers). The reaction is usually one of total shock: "Wow, we knew her for 20 years. We never thought she could have done that in a million years." But by then the damage is already done. So remember the old saying—trust but verify. Too often the owner is an expert in whatever the business does and doesn't have accounting skills. He or she becomes highly dependent on the finance person, and I've seen many scenarios where this finance seat becomes a unicorn with all the passwords and know-how to operate the actual "business" side of the business.

Even if that individual doesn't share the owner's core values and doesn't perform up to par, the business owner and his team end up putting up with a lot of crap because the owner's too dependent on the finance person to let him go. I see this all the time. They've allowed the finance position to become so valuable and powerful that he or she feels like they can do whatever they want unchecked. This is really, *really* unhealthy. The owner often doesn't know what to do because it's a really uncomfortable situation. So the main takeaway here is to make sure to keep an eye on whoever is keeping an eye on the books. Quarterly spot checks and deep annual audits are essential to ensure this process is effective, and make sure the person conducting the audit is not your finance person. It isn't personal, just business.

And this is not just an employee issue. It could be a problem with a vendor or the phone company overcharging you. But if you don't question it and keep writing the checks every month, you're going to lose loads of money. As a small business owner you have to be very diligent in making sure that everything is correct in that department, that you have a procedure to not only check but double-check. Even when you automate something, you have to spot-check it to make sure it's operating at a margin that's good for the business. When I find someone who is a bit lost on their financial state, I recommend to them to sign ALL of the checks for a month or two so they can truly got a concept of what is going out the door at their business. In most cases when they do that a bunch of stuff gets the axe, as they don't see the value, or when they ask around their staff can easily live without whatever was on that monthly schedule.

LESSON 66 ★ Take Care of the Basics

I tell the joke about the "Speed of Payroll," which is somewhere between the speed of light and the speed of sound. If you've ever messed up your payroll, you'll know about it *very fast* because a lot of your employees are leveraged. A $100 or $200 mistake on the business owner's paycheck is usually not a life or death thing, but for some of your more leveraged employees it absolutely is. They have things budgeted and planned for, and they're counting on you to pay them what you said you were going to pay them. Your employees have a really solid expectation of you paying them on time (rightfully so) and when you don't do it, that's a problem. If you ever screw that up on that, you'll hear about it from them maybe even faster than the speed of light.

LESSON 67 ★ Have a System to Understand the Data

If you're making decisions on your gut feeling and not on real, raw data, you're eventually going to get burned. When you have a known system and known numbers and something falls outside of that, you can then manage from a position of clarity. When you put a system in place, it alerts you to problems and allows you to deal with them. If you don't have a system of financial controls in place, you don't know what you don't know.

For those business owners who do require a full-time finance position, I recommend bringing more discipline and accountability into the relationship by getting great weekly scorecard metrics established to avoid any need for concern. Everybody benefits here because great scorecard metrics are vital in every department of your business. For instance, how many accounts receivable calls were made in a given week? It's one thing to know what the number is, it's quite another to know what you're doing every week to make that number move.

If you have $200,000 due to you in accounts receivable that is over 90 days old, what are you doing to get that? How many calls did you make outbound to these clients, checking up on when payment will be made? How many of these outstanding invoices are going to collections? A scorecard is an activities-based metric you can use a week at a time to derive a great business result. If you've got great scorecard metrics, you're then able to spot patterns and trends much sooner than in your monthly financial review. When you're only looking at lagging indicators of things that have already happened, you will always be reactive vs. proactive.

This scorecard is essential to introducing the basic concepts of audit and accountability to all check-signers within your organization. Applying the concept once again of "trust but verify," the bottom line is this: Not everybody in your company should be able to sign a check, and those who are authorized to do so should have introduced into their routine a basic, on-going audit to ensure their accountability for every dime that goes out the door with their name on it. When bad things happen, we always wind up looking at how they were able to happen in the first place, and discover that it's usually due to a lack of controls. The owner's excuse for their naiveté is always something along the lines of: "I never thought this could happen, I trusted this person…" But by then the damage has been done. Another option is to create a tertiary review of all checks that are signed. What that means is, in order for a check to be cut, the expense has to be approved by 2 or 3 people to keep things tight and on track.

So, at the end of the day, you need to let everyone who handles YOUR money know the following: "Hey, we trust you, but we're going to be verifying because it's the responsible business thing to do. No hard feelings, but you're going to be audited in your role. You have to be." A true professional won't take it personally.

 # SAVINGS "BOUNTY" FORM

Finding places to save and paying a 10% commission for 90 days to the employee who found the savings

Name of employee who found the opportunity to cut costs while maintaining quality:
_____

Name of current vendor? _____

Price $ _____ (Per Unit) _____ Currently paying

Terms given? _____

Name of potential new vendor? _____

Price $ _____ (Per Unit) _____ Currently paying

Terms given? _____

How did you find the potential new vendor? _____

How long have they been in business? _____

Are they insured and bonded? _____

What is their online reputation on Google/Yelp or other rating sites? _____

Do you have any experience with them, or do you know someone else who uses them successfully? _____

What is the projected MONTHLY savings from current to new vendor?
_____ X three months = _____

(After 90 days with new vendor, what was the ACTUAL savings from the old vendor?

_____

Actual savings _____ x .10 (to determine the 10% Bounty) = (Bounty amount before payroll taxes and deductions) $ _____

Approved by _____

Bounty paid on next payroll date (Day/Month/Year) _____ / _____ / _____

CHAPTER NINE

Mission Execution (GSD)

"A good plan, violently executed today, is better than a perfect plan executed tomorrow." **—General George Patton**

While starting projects is easy for a lot of people, getting them across the finish line is the tricky part. Just consider the following statistics:

 According to the *Harvard Business Review*, "a recent survey of more than 400 global CEOs found that **EXECUTIONAL EXCELLENCE** was the NUMBER ONE CHALLENGE facing CORPORATE LEADERS in Asia, Europe, and the United States, heading a list of some 80 issues."[52]

 "When we teach strategy to MBAs, **95%** OF THE TIME IS SPENT ON THE **THEORY OF STRATEGY,** while at best **5%** is spent on execution. While in the real world, for the majority of people it is the exact opposite—**5%**, maybe **10%**, is spent on strategy, while **95%** is focused on executing our strategy."[53]

 The Wharton School of Business reports, **"ONCE A PLAN IS DECIDED UPON,** THERE IS OFTEN SURPRISINGLY LITTLE **FOLLOW-THROUGH** TO ENSURE THAT IT IS EXECUTED... a lack of expertise in execution can have serious consequences... Much of that gap between expectation and performance is a failure to execute the company's strategy effectively."[54]

LinkedIn recently reported what they termed the "sad statistic" **90%** OF ORGANIZATIONS FAIL 😊😟😟😟😟😟😟😟😟😟 fail to successfully execute their strategies.[55]

Entrepreneur magazine recently noted, "a lot of organizations put great strategies together but they don't follow through:

 **80%** OF THEM FAIL AT THE EXECUTION PART OF THE STRATEGY."[56]

[52] https://hbr.org/2015/03/why-strategy-execution-unravelsand-what-to-do-about-it
[53] https://www.forbes.com/sites/karlmoore/2012/05/31/strategy-without-execution-is-hallucination
[54] http://knowledge.wharton.upenn.edu/article/three-reasons-why-good-strategies-fail-execution-execution
[55] https://www.linkedin.com/pulse/20140716150513-6557736-why-90-of-organizations-fail-to-successfully-execute-their-strategies
[56] https://www.entrepreneur.com/article/237005

LESSON 68 ★ Execution is Paramount

The bottom line: in business, *execution is paramount!* I believe vision is sold by the pound because there's an unlimited supply of it. Traction or execution is sold by the carat because it's rare and extremely valuable.

The chasm between not being good and being great is huge, and companies that can execute ultimately win because everything else is just talk until it's done. That's the beauty of execution: a small team of A players can run circles around a much larger team of C players. Understanding the market and the quality of your *execution* determine how many referrals you're going to get and your reputation. So it's mission critical.

If your branding is great, your marketing is great, and the sales process was wonderful, but you can't execute once in operations mode, then you have problems. But when you follow all the other steps in this Field Manual, you're creating an environment of consistent and professional execution. If we're talking about anything in this book, we're talking about executing on your vision. To quote an unofficial military acronym, G.S.D. or GET SHIT/STUFF DONE!

Companies that get it done at a high rate enjoy more profit, more growth, and more fun. Companies that can execute consistently can run circles around their competitors. When you're great at execution, you're not afraid to take chances with your business. You can be risky and bold when you know it's likely to get done because that's how we roll in this unit. We usually don't fight battles we don't think we can win, and we definitely don't want to engage in fights we aren't committed to. It's also important to understand that while getting shit done is important, getting the right shit done is really where your head should be. So, think about adopting the term G.R.S.D. If fact, I have a few clients that have adopted G.R.S.D. as a core value, so their employees know it's OK to challenge what they are working on, and is it really moving the needle at your business, or is it just busy work that really doesn't matter in the end.

LESSON 69 ★ High Accountability = High Execution

Execution is a combination of having the right people, the right leadership, and the right culture. When you have a healthy culture, you have an ecosystem in which high levels of accountability exist; if you have a poor culture, there will be low levels of accountability across the board.

High accountability = high execution. It's as simple (and as hard) as that. If we're accountable to each other and have a culture of accountability, when somebody says they're going to do something, it gets done. They're essentially attaching their name and reputation and ability to the execution of the process.

It's well known that people in the military don't generally join for the great pay and easy hours because both suck pretty hard compared to the civilian world. They join because of the greater good, to do something way bigger than just one person. When you have that kind of commitment, accountability is much easier to come by. If your people have a "take it or leave it" mentality where everything is just the same to them, it's nearly impossible to hold them accountable; after all, no one cares!

Forbes noted that accountability is a "discipline is where execution really takes place." By contrast, if we have low levels of accountability, it's really difficult to get strong levels of execution because ultimately we can't see where were supposed to be. Somebody doesn't have their stuff done and no one else is doing anything about it, so you just spin in a circle like the majority of businesses. To combat that, we have to institute what the military likes to call a "G.S.D." culture. Less talk, more action!

In business, we measure real things because we want to know how fast we're moving, and once we get comfortable executing to a certain degree, sometimes we can go a little faster and pick up more velocity. This concept is highlighted in the book *Scrum: The Art of Doing Twice the Work in Half the Time* by Jay Sutherland, who lays out a revolutionary way to get things done.

I work with several software companies that use this methodology to make their products. For example, anyone who has put together an Ikea desk knows that the first one will take you 45 minutes to assemble. But after you know how to do it, you can assemble the rest of them in about half the time. So the idea here is that once you get to know how to do something and get better at it, you can go a little faster. As everyone gets better incrementally, we keep ratcheting up the expectations because they're achievable. And because of our new, higher level of competency, our velocity increases and we're able to accomplish more in a shorter amount of time. So when you have a culture of execution and are always trying to get a little bit better, you end up doing more—whether that's more service, more smiles, or more profits.

The main idea of this whole military mindset is this: The military doesn't generally lower standards. Not everybody gets through Special Forces Selection or Ranger School; that's not how it works. That's why those accomplishments are revered in the Army. They're not easy to get, so that kind of competition breeds the "best-of-the best-mentality" because the bar is set so high. So I'll come back once again to one of the main tenets of this field manual: STOP LOWERING THE BAR. (Have I seared that into your mind yet?) When you do, your business will start to perform at a higher level. Most business owners, for whatever reason, think they can't be this demanding, but the reality is that you usually can and I think you HAVE to be.

When you're asking people to realign with a system they've never followed before, it can be difficult to hold them to that standard. But if some high performers can pave the way in showing others that it's possible, then it's only a matter of time before somebody else can do it too. Most businesses successes are repeatable—you just have to create the conditions for people to want to achieve your goals and be able to do so.

LESSON 70 ★ You Accomplish Goals by Measuring Progress

You commit to being great at executing and getting better at it by tracking how many of your weekly to-dos are getting to-done. Without a system to keep you on track, it's very difficult to get better in this arena.

Scorecards give employees something measurable to aspire to. Whoever said, "whatever can be measured can be managed,"[58] was right on the money, because execution is about visibility, setting a goal, and then tracking your progress toward it until the goal is accomplished.

So for instance, if it's a months-long project without any real check-ins from management, and then the project winds up behind schedule, you need to make a course correction to get it back on track. If you're managing (NOT micromanaging) people and their weekly scorecards alert you that certain things aren't happening, you can step in and intercede before things get too far off the rails.

The Wall Street Journal endorsed and embraced this approach:, "The main requirements for successful execution are: 1) clear goals for everyone in the organization, that are supportive of the overall strategy; 2) a means of measuring progress toward those goals on a regular basis; and 3) clear accountability for that progress. Those are the basics… If there is a common understanding among everyone in the room on goals and timelines, and if all

---

[58] This is commonly attributed to Peter Drucker, but that's not confirmed.

leave the room with a clear sense of what needs to happen next and who needs to do it, then you are likely witnessing a strong culture of execution."[59]

But if you expect perfection right off the bat, you're expecting the wrong thing. Your expectation should be that your employees aren't perfect, yet you can still set the bar to a high level and there's no reason why 80% to 90% of the expectations you set can't be accomplished. Set whatever number is comfortable for your organization, but make sure it isn't a number like 50%. When your expectations are set that low, your employees will never measure up.

Once we make a decision, we must execute—it's that simple. First you have to decide where you want to go and what you want to do, then you formulate a plan to do it and simply follow through. Most people have heard the term "backwards military planning." This isn't that the plan is the opposite of what you would do in the civilian world, but first setting your end objective or desired result, then planning backward from there.

For example: We need to go kick a door down and grab a really bad guy at 0500. We will be at the rally point at 0430, draw weapons at 0415, eat chow and brief at 0400, and wake up at 0315. There will be learning opportunities along the way and chances to course-correct where necessary, but if you don't have a plan, and your end game is a difficult one, don't be surprised if you don't entirely meet your objectives. But if you apply a military-grade business execution, you can put together a plan that makes sense, anticipates contingencies, ensures you have the right resources, and, most importantly, has the right people in the right places at exactly the right time. Everyone on your team knows precisely what their individual roles and responsibilities are. When you do that, your chances of executing to a higher standard are obviously much greater.

There's a strong mindset of execution in the military, a culture of being laser-focused on completing tasks—whether it's in combat, a peacekeeping mission, in a training school, or ongoing training within a unit. It starts with basic training, where they take civilians and turn them into soldiers, and everyone is in it together. You can do the same in business—training builds confidence as a unit and that kind of culture spreads throughout the team's mentality: "We can do *anything* we put our minds and attention to!"

By building that sense of confidence slowly and surely, your team will be fired up and eager to fight the bigger battles and take on the larger tasks together because they've already successfully navigated through all the basic and intermediate stuff. Little wins, one after the other, build upon each other until

[59] http://guides.wsj.com/management/execution/what-are-the-keys-to-good-execution

they create the mindset of being a champion, who of course wins a lot of the time. That history of accomplishment will breed the confidence to guarantee better execution. Once you've been to the end zone a few times and believe you can score again, you'll look at a mission that's really difficult to accomplish and say, "with this team, we can ABSOLUTELY do that!"

LESSON 71 ★ Having a Scorecard Will Root out the "Hiders"

Quite often in my coaching I see teams full of people who really think they're great executors, or because they're the best executors on a team of poor executors they set the bar for the rest of the team and it isn't a very high one. I've seen employees like this at almost every company I've worked with, but as soon as you put a weekly scorecard in place, these people voluntarily opt out of the company—and I mean *quickly*. As soon as a scorecard makes their performance (or lack of it) visible, they will instinctively run for the hills. Accountability is something your A players won't mind because it validates their "A" status, but it's the C players who have something to worry about: their social capital at the business had become more valuable than their execution capital.

I call these people *"The Hiders."* These are people who, usually for social reasons, have nothing to do with their work product. They're continually allowed to skirt their responsibilities because they're fun to talk to, tell great jokes, give great compliments, or they're good at golf. Whatever it is, they're doing half the workload of someone who doesn't have those qualities. The hider is often viewed as the better employee, when in fact other members of their team are actually doing a lot more work.

In the smaller businesses I deal with there are a lot less places to hide, but you'd be surprised— even in a small company with 20 or 30 people you can still have three or four hiders, and they can really make a huge difference in how that organization functions. That behavior is so much more costly to a small business and touches a larger percentage of their customer base. If somebody doesn't have a number to hit, that person is simply not producing at their peak capacity. This is even a bigger problem in larger companies where there are way more places to hide.

This is what a weekly scorecard does for you—it provides the return loop, so you can see who's working hard and who isn't. Wouldn't that be great? In most companies there's just the standard agreement with the employee—as long as you're paying them they keep showing up, but with that approach you're really just writing checks and accepting whatever they decide to give you.

How can you be sure you're getting a good return on your investment? How are we tracking those "return" metrics, so it's not just a one-way street of a paycheck and no deliverables or measurables from the employee? Now, if that employee is in a sales position with commission-based pay, you're much more likely to know exactly who's over-performing vs. under-performing. But in other roles it's more difficult to track performance and your lagging employees can more easily hide among the masses. They may not be pulling their numbers but you still have to pay them, and that's wrong.

The beauty of the scorecard is that it levels the playing field for all, putting aside social and behavioral considerations and putting the focus on a handful of indiscriminate (and non-emotional) numbers. The numbers almost never lie, so when we start relying more on empirical data and less on gut feeling, we're able to make much better decisions for the organization. A business can't afford to have huge swings in productivity from one team member to the next.

When I work with businesses that aren't holding their employees accountable with scorecards, I always go right to the heart of the problem, which is typically that management is aware of the behavior but is not doing anything to address it. I probe this problem with basic questions:

- Is there a Letter of Reprimand in their personnel file?

- Are you giving them time off without pay?

- Are you docking their bonus or reconsidering their annual pay increase?

- Have you started a paper trail?

In most cases there's a bunch of mumbling and a lot of excuses: "Well, it's hard to get people," or, "I'd love to fire this person but they know a lot of stuff," etc. So a lot of times that leader figures, "Even if this person isn't executing at high standards, they're still executing at *some* level and I'd be remiss to change that." It's poisonous for a business to have the mentality of "it's cheaper to keep her" and accepting whatever the employee bothers to deliver. That apathetic view is why 70% of Americans are disengaged at work—because 70% of *bosses* in America don't understand their role in helping people be successful.

This is where I give EOS®, my favorite business operating system, a huge amount of credit, because the system is basically set up to create a grand vision, put the right people in the right seats, give everybody a measurable scorecard number to be held accountable to, and forge an environment where problems or issues can be discussed and addressed in an open, honest, and healthy fashion. This is the process for how you get tasks accomplished. You have a schedule where people are consistently checking in; you're NOT micromanaging your staff and breathing down their necks every day, but having a weekly meeting where you make sure the strategic issues and scorecard numbers are on track. If you're doing that consistently by keeping the same meeting schedule every week, it creates an environment where a huge spotlight is directed on the people who aren't executing.

LESSON 72 ★ Always Be Prepared to Have a Difficult Conversation

If you're an owner or leader who's half committed, it will become obvious to everyone around you really fast. By the same token, if you're an owner or leader who's 100% committed and you're tolerating people in your lineup who aren't, you need to bench them until they are committed or cut them from the squad entirely. When your operating system indicates it's time to fire, then you need to fire. You just have to pull the trigger, period. The rules of engagement are as follows: If someone in the organization no longer shares or lives your core values, or no longer gets, wants, or has the capacity to do the job, then you need to have a tough conversation. If they share your core values but just aren't the right person for that seat, maybe there's a more suitable position we can find for them elsewhere in the company. But if they're the wrong person and don't share your values, it doesn't matter what position you put them in; they're still in the wrong unit. You never want to destroy your hard-earned *esprit de corps*. That person will be much happier once they find their right unit.

I've seen this over and over again, whether it's a people issue or a process issue or a customer issue. For whatever reason, the entrepreneur or leader lacks the confidence to cut the cord. Occasionally, but still very rare, that's a legitimate view if your faltering employee has a certain technical expertise that's key to your company's operation. But even then you can't let them abuse their value to you. More businesses operate in a commodity space than in a specialist space, so if you have a large hiring pool to pick from, why hang on to dead weight when you don't need to?

According to Gallup, "Companies fail to choose the candidate with the right talent for the job 82% of the time. Managers account for at least 70% of variance in employee engagement scores across business units. Performance metrics fluctuate widely and unnecessarily in most companies, in no small part from the lack of consistency in how people are managed. This 'noise' frustrates leaders because unpredictability causes great inefficiencies in execution."[60]

So when behavior is in conflict with your company's mission, and you've communicated how important your vision is when you asked your team to fully commit, then you need to step up and protect that vision whenever it's threatened. If you're avoiding being a strong leader for fear of having a difficult conversation, then maybe you shouldn't be sitting at the head of the conference table.

The military rarely tolerates non-performers in critical roles. They're relieved of duty and assigned to a position that requires minimal responsibility until their time is up or they get chaptered out early. As a Business Sergeant you need to dig deep and let your team see you lead by executing again and again with military precision.

To execute at your best, create incentives for people to reach your company's goals. You don't want your pay plan to be the reason why they're not executing. At the same time, Inc. magazine makes the compelling point, "we all know the problems associated with underpaying—lack of motivation, high turnover, and general disgruntledness. But what about the problems with overpaying? … When salaries are too high, people start to believe that this is what they are entitled to. And it actually discourages hard work, because they're already getting the reward… as they become slackers, they become more and more satisfied with their comfy and cushy jobs."[61]

You commit to being great by making personnel moves commensurate with implementing scorecards and enhancing accountability. Once your A players see the dead weight offloaded, they will take the culture of execution more seriously. Once they see you making big moves that you wouldn't have made before, see your commitment and passion to making the company great, they'll be more apt to opt in. All great Business Sergeants know that showing them is almost always easier and effective than telling them.

Once you have that full buy-in from your team, you've liberated the hiders and cut loose the dead weight. You're making decisions based on culture over profit for the long term. That level of commitment from the owner will be reflected back by your employees. Cleaning house gets us where we want to go much faster, even if it seems a little abrupt or uncaring at first. You're saving yourself and your team a lot of unnecessary pain in the long run. Would you

[60] http://www.gallup.com/businessjournal/167975/why-great-managers-rare.aspx
[61] https://www.inc.com/suzanne-lucas/are-you-paying-your-employees-too-much.html

rather rip the Band-Aid off and scream for a couple seconds? Or pull it off slowly and scream for 30 seconds? As a strong Business Sergeant, you want to inspire your team to execute by leading through example, which means not punting on the tough calls, being clear about your expectations, and maintaining a culture that produces extraordinary results.

LESSON 73 ★ Plan by Quarters and Rely on Rocks

One thing I've learned from my friend Gino Wickman is that people have about 90 days of attention span. I see this in myself; when I look back at my career, I think, "Wow, I really should have segmented my goals into quarters. I would have been a lot more effective in reaching them." Planning by quarters allows you to get an overview of the bigger goals—the goals that are 1 year, 3 years, and 10 years out. It makes it a lot easier to reach those goals by creating a 90-Day World™, having everyone execute within that 90-Day World™, and then have everyone re-enlist for another 90 days of mission execution.

I've heard it said that an employee's first 90 days at a company will be that employee's greatest contribution, meaning they'll put in their greatest level of effort. We live in a world where 70% of managers aren't very good and 70% of employees are disengaged at work. Those two numbers go hand in hand. It's because employees figure out after 90 days that their manager doesn't really care about them. That's when disengagement and lack of commitment start to show. You don't want a company that suffers that fate.

Once you've established a 3-Year Picture™ with the right people in the right seats for what you want to accomplish, you start with a 1-Year Plan™ That 1-year plan is a lead domino—what do you need to get rolling to put yourself on the right trajectory? That in turn leads us to our quarterly *Rocks* or what we call strategic initiatives, something outside the day-to-day business that, once completed, gives your company new capability and new capacity. Humans have about 90 days of attention span, so by creating a 90-Day World™ with Rocks, you develop the capacity to do business every quarter and then we move on to the next one. These 90-day periods are very, very powerful; if we're executing at a very high percentage—80% or better—then we're fundamentally changing the company and going beyond where we were yesterday.

FOCUS ON THE CLIENT
World Class Execution at Umbrella Roofing

Trevor Cannon runs a high-end roofing company in the most expensive zip codes of the Rocky Mountains in Colorado ski country. His company is very profitable, with a huge market share and a crazy backlog. These guys just execute, but in the year-and-a-half I worked with them, they got better at G.S.D.

Last year they thought they were going to have a slow winter building roofs, so they shifted to snow removal from roofs and blew up their numbers! Multi-millionaire homeowners don't like excuses, so Umbrella Roofing's schedule is full because his company executes consistently, day in and day out. When they say they're going to be there at 8, they're there at 8. Their core values are listed on each installer's shirt and because of their culture they have a low turnover.

In short, they are the most functional roofing company I've ever seen, and usually roofing is controlled chaos, roofers being the red-headed step children of the construction industry. But not these guys!

Here's what Trevor had to say about our work together:

The best part about having Chris work with us is that it enabled me, as the owner, to sit on the same side of the table as the management team. I wasn't sitting on the opposite side of the table telling management what to do or imposing goals on them. Instead, I sat there and kept my mouth shut and let these guys talk. I don't think they were really that nervous around me anyway, but it has changed our dynamic in a positive way.

We were already pretty good at calling each other out, but I think the greatest help was giving us the EOS® process that provides much more structure and more organization. We were already doing annual meetings throughout the year, but our meetings with Chris have been very powerful for us. You know your issue's going to be addressed and that it's there for everybody to see, and while we haven't totally taken the emotion out of it, we've come a long way towards doing that.

One of the biggest changes for us has been a defined agenda for weekly meetings. This has dramatically reduced the hallway meetings, the talking between people. Now everyone knows they're going to have a chance to talk at the weekly meeting, so there's no need to talk outside of that.

As a result, our productivity as managers has really improved.

We were already a pretty vision-oriented company, but now we have the framework to put that vision down in a clearly defined manner, in a really clear framework—how we're going to execute over 1-year, 3-year, and 10-year periods.

What will be the process for each period? This framework has produced great results for us.

We had five years in a row with an average growth of 34% a year, from 2011 through 2015. Our systems were strained, and when you're that busy it's hard to take a step back and redesign or beef up the systems you have. We pretty much knew we were maxed out with what we could do in our capacity. And without figuring it out, we couldn't just grow for the sake of growing. We had to implement some structure, better systems, and better lines of communication to facilitate any further growth.

The Accountability Chart™ has been great in forcing us to think about how we were structured initially and about how we want to be structured in the future. And having goals you have to hit every three months really helps to keep the pressure up. You know what the goal is, everybody sees it, and we talk about it every single week. We know whether we're on track or off track, so it keeps the pressure on us to make progress and do better.

✪ THE LEVEL 10 MEETING™ AGENDA

Most business meetings are an epic waste of time. Without a set agenda and the discipline and focus to stay on track, you're probably not getting as much done as you should. This tool can help you change that.

The Level 10 Meeting™ Agenda from EOS® is a very powerful format that will keep your meetings at a very high level, so you can hold fewer meetings, and get more done. To learn more about EOS® and The Level 10 Meeting™ Agenda, please visit www.eosworldwide.com or download their app (keyword: EOS Worldwide)

THE LEVEL 10 MEETING™

The Weekly Agenda

Day: _____   Time: _____

Agenda:

Segue	5 Minutes
Scorecard	5 Minutes
Rock Review	5 Minutes
Customer/Employee Headlines	5 Minutes
To-Do List	5 Minutes
IDS	60 Minutes

Conclude
    Recap To-Do List
    Cascading messages
    Rating (1-10)
	5 Minutes

EOS®
Entrepreneurial Operating System®

SIMPLIFIED BUSINESS OPERATIONS ORDER

Exactly how we will get something done with a cool plan B (modified from U.S. Army)

The military uses standardized formats for many different things, including when training or live operation is approved to begin. Before starting, you must plan in great detail to ensure a high level of success can be achieved. This planning process is called an OPORD or Operational Order. Like everything else in the military, there is an acronym to remember everything you must do to properly complete an OPORD. The acronym is S.M.E.S.C. or (Sergeant Majors Eat Sugar Cookies for easy recall)

S = Situation **M** = Mission **E** = Execution **S** = Service Support **C** = Command & Signal

Here is my business-adapted version of a traditional military OPORD (BIZ-OPORD):

S. Situation

1. External Business (Client/Prospect name)_____

  a. Location _____

  b. Business Activity _____

  c. # of Employees _____ Reputation in the market _____

  d. Probable Needs and Wants _____

2. Friendly Forces (Referral source or Partners)_____

  a. Missions of Friendly Forces (Referral source or Partners) _____

  b. Current actions of Friendly Forces _____

M. Mission

Who: _____

What: _____

Where: _____

Why: _____

When: _____

E. Execution

1. Leader's Intent: _____

2. Concept of the Operation _____

   a. Who is leading this Operation? _____

   b. Do we have a warm or cold introduction? (Name/Relationship if Warm)

   _____

   c. Names of team members on this operation and their specific roles _____

   _____

   d. What resources will we need? (Presentations, research, tools, samples, reports etc.)

   _____

   e. Rehearsal schedule for: _____

   f. Debriefing/ After Action Review Scheduled for: _____

S. Service Support

1. Who is providing necessary resources?_____

2. What is the deadline for assembling the Resources? _____

3. Who is bringing resources? _____

4. Who is booking transportation? (If any) _____

5. Who is booking accommodations? (If any) _____

6. What is the dress code for this operation? (Can be multiple uniforms) _____

_____

C. Command and Signal

1. Chain of Command 1._____ 2. _____

   3._____ 4. _____

2. Duties and location of Leader(s) during Operation _____

3. Methods of communication for operation? _____

4. Reporting requirements during operation?_____

The time is _____ What are your questions?

CHAPTER TEN

You'll Need Some Help!

"Companies that do not have the revenue to justify paying someone a six-figure salary may consider hiring someone to play the role part time."[62]

—The New York Times

In the military, there's a long-held credo that weaves its way throughout every branch of service—a unit is only as strong as the weakest soldier. To create that culture of reliable execution among your team of troops, you must start with the notion of loyalty to your company's vision, core values, and culture.

But even when you have your core unit together, you'll need to reach out to others for assistance to successfully execute your mission. This approach happens all the time in the armed forces. A unit in a war zone will often work with a K-9 bomb-sniffing specialist, for example. The Army, Navy, Air Force, and Marines have to work together in seamless coordination of their specialized skill-sets to successfully pull off complex major operations.

You will need to find the same kind of expert help to complement your in-house expertise. Our armed forces are often augmented by government contractors; in the same way, you will need outside help. If you're a seasonal business, you'll need extra bodies to help with holiday orders. You might even find yourself calling in extra help for two or three departments simultaneously, making it even more crucial to have these external strategic partnerships in place. There's very little downside to this kind of investment.

The bottom line is this: The quality of the units you attach to yours will make a HUGE difference in the fight you bring to the market. In doing this, you can follow the age-old adage of not paying 100% or taking on a full-time cost if you only have a part-time need. If you're not the expert, simply hire one on a part-time basis. For instance, if you can't afford full-time legal counsel,

 [62] http://www.nytimes.com/2011/10/27/business/smallbusiness/when-should-a-small-business-hire-a-chief-financial-officer.html

hire a freelance attorney who comes in one day a week to do the contract and compliance reviews at your business.

SMART CEO.com highlights the benefits you can derive from this approach: "Cost containment is a major driver in most outsourcing decisions, but many other benefits exist as well, including improved efficiencies, greater sense of business continuity, mitigating risk by leveraging specialists, and freeing staff to focus on core services and strategy."[63]

LESSON 74 ★ Carefully Screen and Monitor Outside Vendors

In linking up with strategic partners, it's crucial to make sure they share your mission vision and values. This way, your employees and customers won't feel much difference between working with them vs. working directly with you. It's critical to be VERY CAREFUL about which outside vendors you allow to have direct or indirect access to your clients, whether we're talking about subcontractors or agencies that represent your brand in the market. It's crucial that they're not saying or doing things that stand in direct conflict with whatever you have promised the client. They are representing you, and the client won't make the distinction when they leave you for a competitor because the outside vendor didn't deliver. The continuity should be seamless, so much so that the customer is never able to tell the difference between whether they're talking to someone who works directly for your company, or to an outsourced vendor or partner. It's important to ensure that the caliber and quality of your external partners' employee teams are as solid as your own.

When you need to ramp up with extra people who share your values, who understand how you do business, you can just flip that switch and not have to worry. It's incredibly liberating as a business owner to have the capacity to augment your labor force as needed and not have it be a huge headache of hiring and firing. This keeps your core team tighter because they're receiving the proper support and maintaining unit cohesion. Then, once you've met demand, you can shrink the size of that external work force with no hard feelings or disruptions to your core inner unit.

LESSON 75 ★ Learn to Delegate

Many business owners have trouble letting go of control. They're unable to delegate down the chain. Wearing too many hats can have dangerous consequences. D.I.Y. is the natural culture of a small business, but sometimes doing it yourself will take twice the time and aggravation, and probably twice the cost. That's why it's important to reach out to strategic partners who are experts in their specific fields. They will save you headaches, time, and most importantly money. Successfully buying into this concept as a business owner requires some measure of trust. The beauty here is you can purchase piece of mind by hiring companies you've researched thoroughly, not only by referral but through your own interviewing process. You can apply the same system of core values as when hiring one of your own internal employees. This helps guarantee all-important continuity with your customers as we discussed before, and frees you up to focus on running your company from your greatest position of strength. The company will be stronger as a result.

As a business owner or leader, you *have* to become a Jack-of-all-Trades. But after a while you become so used to being in control of so many things that you have a hard time delegating, even when it *works against you not to.* Entrepreneurs are supposed to be great problem solvers by nature, great simplifiers, and this has to extend to you as an asset of the business as well.

I'm happy to let the smart folks at the *Harvard Business Review* make this argument for me:

> "We've spent the past three years studying how knowledge workers can become more productive and found that the answer is simple: Eliminate or delegate unimportant tasks and replace them with value-added ones. Our research indicates that knowledge workers spend a great deal of their time—an average of 41%—on discretionary activities that offer little personal satisfaction and could be handled competently by others... The goal, of course, is to be not just efficient but effective. So the next step is to determine how to best make use of the time you've saved. Write down two or three things you should be doing but aren't, and then keep a log to assess whether you're using your time more effectively. Some of our study participants were able to go home a bit earlier to enjoy their families (which probably made them happier and more productive the next day)."[64]

LESSON 76 ★ Sub-Contract Services When Possible

Another asset to having strong strategic partners is that you don't have to give prospective clients the dreaded "no" when they come to you for a service you don't directly offer. When you have strategic partnerships already in place,

[64] https://hbr.org/2013/09/make-time-for-the-work-that-matters

your answer can be "ABSOLUTELY, we CAN help you with that!" You can either pass a referral on to a trusted partner for a referral fee, or sub-contract out whatever that needed service is, instead of possibly losing your initial sale as many clients these days want a sole source solution. You can charge a competitive rate that is fair to both you and the contractor, and this saves the customer the headache of having to look somewhere else when they're already happy doing business with you. In the Business Sergeant headspace, there's always room for strategic partners to augment your forces. I'm not suggesting that you become a jack-of-all-trades, and subcontract anything you can. That would be a big mistake. What I am talking about is augmenting your forces to help with what you already do well, or those things that are complementary to your services and make sense from a Core Focus™ perspective (the task is very close to your company's sweet spot)

Keeping consistent strategic partnerships is vital, not only to keeping the customer happy, but your own team members as well. Building working relationships with outside vendors will enable your entire ship to run more smoothly.

One you establish strategic partnerships, commit to using them for as long as they provide value. If you're constantly switching strategic partnerships, A) your staff has to constantly adjust to the learning curve of a new relationship, and B) this creates an atmosphere where everyone's coming and going, tripping over each other. So don't do a lot of flip-flopping; it's just plain dangerous for all parties involved.

LESSON 76 ★ Regularly Evaluate Your Strategic Partnerships

At the same time, you don't want to become too complacent and fail to monitor and periodically evaluate your strategic partners. There's always a honeymoon period with a new vendor, but over time anyone can get a little lazy, a little sleepy, putting a lot of effort into their new clients while assuming you'll be with them forever. In making that assumption, they might take some liberties, whether with pricing, service, etc. So just as you do with your employees, review your external units every quarter.

Re-evaluate the relationship every 90 days just like you do wither your employees, ask them to recommit, and then move forward for another quarter. Even if you have signed a 1-year contract, I still recommend the quarterly conversation with your vendor to make sure you're communicating your needs to them and they're hearing you. Once you're in a happy place where you have clear expectations and they're being met, you can go into maintenance mode while making sure that the service is being executed to the standard you originally set. Always maintain open channels of communication with potential new vendors in case an existing relationship does go sour right when you need to service a new client. This way you have back-up partners on the bench that you can put into play.

LESSON 77 ★ Free Up the Business Leader's Time

The other beauty of these relationships as a business owner is that it frees you up to go home and spend time with your loved ones, so you can keep your home life as healthy as your business. In contrast, overworked entrepreneurs and business owners who have families at home but are wearing too many hats will suffer both personally and professionally in the long run.

Entrepreneur magazine cautions that small business owners "are often celebrated for wearing multiple hats and logging numerous hours. But working without letup is a bad habit that can jeopardize business, health, and the life you're supposedly working toward. It's easy to fall into the trap of overdoing it, since capital in the early days is tight, but also because few ambitious achievers understand one of the biggest secrets of productivity—the refueling principle."[65] If you have a family at home you're providing for, you have to remember that kids only grow up once and you can't put a price on that time.

We will explore this concept in much greater depth in the next chapter, but when your business is working well, you can offload certain tasks and services—whether internally or externally—so you can do what you're best at, which is being a good parent and spouse. In the words of Don Corleone in *The Godfather*: "A man who doesn't spend time with his family can never be a real man." That's old-school advice and important to remember as you choose strategic partners who can take the load off you at work.

Remember that augmenting your unit with reinforcements from outside is much faster than training a new platoon of privates. You'll be expanding your capabilities and adding new areas of expertise in your company, while saving time and money in the process. It's just smart thinking and smart business, and the neat thing about outsourcing is that you can dabble in other product lines and markets by using the outside unit's resources and skills.

[65] https://www.entrepreneur.com/article/237446

By the same token, if you're thinking of adding a new department internally for a service you're currently outsourcing, working with that strategic partner may give you a bird's eye view of the costs or management challenges of adding that new department. It may be cheaper and safer to stick with the strategic partner than doing it yourself.

LESSON 78 ★ Seek Out Industry Associations

It's important for entrepreneurs to surround themselves with people who are experiencing the same professional challenges. This is one of the biggest recommendations I can make and I'll say it over and over again—joining an association can make a HUGE difference in how you run your business, from connecting with new potential clients and strategic partners, to just making friends with people who face the same small business problems day in and out. They can offer insight, advice, a laugh, or just an ear to lessen the stress.

Entrepreneur Magazine recently pointed out that, "a good business mentor can offer his or her own experience to help you project future sales, and even offer historical sales figures from personal experience to help you predict upcoming sales volumes."[66]

I've been a member of industry associations for many years, and those groups have really helped me understand what it means to be a small business owner. When you can find 100 other people in the same city who are in the same position as you are, whatever their specific industry might be, the assistance they can offer is invaluable. Some of my best new business ideas have come out of conversations with other entrepreneurs in this type of social setting. There are LOTS of industry groups out there, so find the one that is right for you and never look back.

Another thing I've noticed is that my clients who are members of industry associations are dealing with the rigors of being an entrepreneur a bit better than those who go it alone. When you're the top brass at your business, it's very difficult to have someone at the company who truly understands what's it like to be "the general." Joining an industry association is one of the biggest game changers for a business leader, as a lot of the members of the industry group are business leaders, and know what it's like is to walk in your combat boots.

[66] https://www.entrepreneur.com/article/249020

There are many reasons for a business owner to join an industry association:

- Heavy is the head that wears the crown—other top leaders will "get you."

- You will meet people who are passionate about improving themselves and their companies (not a bad pack to run with).

- They will have vetted resources for you to use, and they will provide advice and experience you would never be exposed to otherwise.

If you've ever spoken with an entrepreneur who is an active member of an industry group, he or she will mostly likely give HUGE amounts of credit to their industry association for their success. Most of us have no idea of what we don't know; getting involved in an industry association is an effective way to find out!

Simply said, being an entrepreneur or business leader is *really*, really hard! The ability to learn from others is truly priceless. It certainly was in my case. I can't recommend joining a industry association strongly enough. In fact, industry associations are a great resource where you can find vetted strategic partners others in the association have used with success, taking a bit of risk away. In the next and final chapter, I'll talk about peer-to-peer groups, that are usually industry agnostic, and focus on the entrepreneur or business leader rather than the industry. I think you need both kinds of support to be your very best.

FOCUS ON THE CLIENT
Building Strategic Partnerships at Advision Marketing

One of the most eloquent spokespeople for the power of strategic partnerships is Matt Walde, president of Advision Marketing. I'll let Matt describe how we worked together:

I had joined an organization called EO, Entrepreneurs Organization, three years ago. It's a network of entrepreneurs who are all in similar situations—we were crazy for starting our own businesses and we share experiences. If I'm facing a challenge I'm trying to figure out, someone in this network is probably going to have a similar story or experience that can help me with my problem.

AdVision was five people when I joined EO and we were doing about $500,000–$600,000 a year in revenue. At one EO meeting, Chris put on a presentation that was part EOS® and part of his own mindset and methodologies. He was a military man, he had been a prison guard, he was very firm in his ways, and I knew immediately that's what our group needed. Because we were five marketers without much of a business structure, much of anything.

At the time, we had a small- company mindset. We knew we were starting something cool, but we were grinding very much. We were self-starters and we were going to do everything on our own—develop our own tools and systems and marketing. I had started the business with a laptop that my parents bought me.

Chris opened our minds to the idea that strategic partnerships weren't an admission that we couldn't do things ourselves. He taught us was that by investing a little bit of money and finding a partner who specialized in an area of our business, we would accelerate that part of the business far beyond what we were capable of doing internally. At the same time, this frees your time to focus on what you're exceptionally good at.

For example, one of the partnerships he suggested was with a company called PayScale, which provides compensation values for different roles and different size organizations across the country. So instead of me spending time trying to figure out what I should be paying our people, I was instead able to focus on growing our agency. Yes, it costs a little money to find an expert to help you, but it's going to be well worth it in the long run.

We got out of that small-business mindset of, "we're only five people, we can't afford a partner, we can't afford to pay anyone, we have to do everything ourselves." I think that's a very common mindset for anyone who starts a business from ground zero.

A company of any size can and should leverage the expertise of individuals, of partners, or of other companies that have specific knowledge in an area where you lack. It seems common sense, but it wasn't to us at the time. You can streamline your job to free up time so you can focus on the most valuable activities in your company.

Another was 15Five, a platform that enables me to communicate one-on-one with everyone in our company. Every week they have a survey. How am I feeling this week on a scale of one to five? What are my biggest challenges? What were my goals? How close did I come to completing those goals? What do I want to see the company to do more of? What do I want the company to stop doing? This enables me to get real-time feedback from everyone in the company every week around what the agency is doing well and where we need to improve.

Just as I need to understand the experiences of my employees and be able to communicate with them one-on-one, I also need to keep tabs on the experiences of our clients. A tool that we picked up was Client Heartbeat. It sends out a four-question survey once a quarter and enables clients to rate us as an agency in four different areas. They then take our scores and rank us against other agencies in our area. It's an incredibly valuable gauge as to how we're doing relative to other agencies.

So what Chris forced me to do was to identify my highest value activities in the agency and to free up my time to concentrate on them—taking care of our people, creating a great culture, making sure our clients are having great experiences, and growing the agency. I was wasting my time and the company's money developing compensation strategies and bonus strategies.

Forging strategic partnerships has reduced the noise in my head. That might be the simplest way to put it. As a business leader, you have so many different things going through your brain at any given moment.

The more complex the company becomes, the more you get sucked into that noise and lose sight of priorities. You need to minimize as much of the insignificant noise as you can.

Now I spend more time thinking about and working on the business.

When we started this process, we were around $600,000 in annual revenue. The next year we did over $1.1 million, so from 2015 to 2016 we grew 94%. This year we should do around $1.4 million in revenue with a very nice profit.

A large part of the reason for that growth was that strategic partnerships helped me to focus more clearly on what I needed to be doing within the business. And we're performing at a higher level because of that.

Yes, you're going to be spending more money up front, but strategic alliances are going to make your business better in the long run.

STRATEGIC PARTNER SELECTION WORKSHEET

How to pick the right one for your business; how to spot the wrong ones up front

Vendor _____

What exactly do we need them do for us? _____

_____

Have we been referred? _____ By who? _____

What was their experience with the partner? _____

Rate your initial impression after your first meeting? _____

Do they have the required experience to serve your clients at a high level? _____

Have you discussed your core values with them, and can they adopt them when working with you and your clients? _____

Are they competitively priced? _____ What is the negotiated rate? _____

Have they agreed and committed to your expected timeline to execute their service? _____

What is the protocol for feedback and how will they handle it? _____

Who will be your point of contact? _____

Who is the manager or supervisor assigned to your account? _____

_____

If there is a problem or breach of service expectations what is the agreed upon recourse? (How will they make it right?) _____

—— Rate the following on a 1 to 10 scale (10 being the best): ——

Online reviews/reputation _____   Price _____   Availability _____

Insurance/Bonding _____   Quality _____   Value _____

Your gut feel _____

90-DAY STRATEGIC PARTNER REVIEW

Making sure we are still a great fit together.

Date Range _____ / _____ / _____ to _____ / _____ / _____

Partner reviewed _____

— Rate the following on a 1 to 10 scale (10 being the best): —

Overall Satisfaction . . . . _____

Quality of work . . . . _____

Quality of Customer service . . . . _____

Mistakes/Errors . . . . _____

Compared to other similar vendors that you've used . . . . _____

Communication . . . . _____

Billing accuracy . . . . _____

Feedback from your clients and employees . . . . _____

Would you refer this partner to another . . . . _____

Capacity to take more work from you . . . . _____

Add up total score from 10 areas

TOTAL

90 to 100 = You've got a good one, let's keep it going!

80 to 90 = You're getting decent service;
please address any scores under an 8.

70 to 80 = Reconsider this relationship, you deserve better!

Under 70 = Find another partner immediately.

CHAPTER ELEVEN

Take Care of #1

"What surprises me most is Man, because he sacrifices his health in order to make money. Then he sacrifices money to recuperate his health. And then he is so anxious about the future that he doesn't enjoy the present; the result being he doesn't live in the present or the future; he lives as if he's never going to die, and then he dies having never really lived."

—Dalai Lama

One of the truest and most powerful quotes I've ever heard reads as follows: "The amount of time you spend with your children when they're young determines the amount of time they will spend with you when you're old." That's a deep concept, and one that I hope sinks in by the time you're done reading this chapter. While I've hammered away at the focus you need as an entrepreneur or business leader to make your vision become a reality, the lesson saved for last is also the most important one: you also need to take your focus OFF your business and put it ON your life away from the office.

Huh? That's right, and it's the same philosophy that drove the military to create the concept of leave time so a soldier could leave the battlefield to spend quality time back home with his or her loved ones. With leave, soldiers could function much more effectively and would not forget what they were fighting for. There are a million studies to back up why a healthy business depends on a healthy work force—and I mean mentally, physically, and emotionally healthy—and the risks we can all fall prey to as business owners and leaders when we work so hard that we lose sight of why we're working. God knows that I've done it myself.

Entrepreneurs and business leaders are often hard-wired to be overachievers, and your passion naturally drives you to invest everything into your professional life. Maybe you don't think twice about it, but you need to give it a second thought because of the impact that can have on your employees and your family. Consider what the experts have to say on the subject:

- According to a recent survey of 971 employees, four in 10 U.S. workers finished 2013 with unused paid time off, leaving an average of 3.2 days still on the table.[67]

- CNN points out that the "the power of a vacation" helps U.S. workers "return to 'real life' with a renewed sense of excitement."[68]

- *The New York Times:* "Social scientists who study families and work say that men…who take an early hands-on role in their children's lives are likely to be more involved for years to come and that their children will be healthier."[69]

- The American Psychological Association concluded, "long hours at work increase work-family conflict and that this conflict is in turn related to depression and other stress-related health problems."[70]

- "Workaholics aren't heroes… They don't save the day, they just use it up. The real hero is already home because she figured out a faster way to get things done."[71]

Despite of the truth of these statistics, entrepreneurs are the only people I know who will gladly work 100 hours a week to avoid working 40 hours at a J.O.B. watching the clock and counting the hours. That said, if you're working 80+ hours a week and spending no time with your family, that's not a very good blend either. Even if you're not pissing and moaning about the long hours, your family is surely unhappy about it. You might be having fun putting all your time in at your business, but your kids aren't having fun at home missing those precious couple of hours with you in the evening.

No doubt this is a challenge to do, even as *Entrepreneur* magazine notes, "leaving the work at work is one of the most important recovery strategies— and the hardest. If you're still obsessing about work when you're off the job, no recovery can take place."[72] This is the same for your work staff, who might start to resent it if you're requiring the same time commitment out of them.

[67] http://www.projecttimeoff.com/sites/default/files/PTO_Assessment_Report_1.pdf
[68] http://www.cnn.com/2011/HEALTH/05/24/vacation.mental.benefits
[69] https://www.nytimes.com/2014/11/09/upshot/paternity-leave-the-rewards-and-the-remaining-stigma.html
[70] http://www.apa.org/monitor/jun02/employees.aspx
[71] *Rework* by David Heinemeier Hansson and Jason Fried, Crown Business, 2010
[72] https://www.entrepreneur.com/article/237446

If you're a leader and owner, you have to remember you're responsible for other people and their balance as well.

Sometimes you have to stay late to keep the business running, but it shouldn't be the rule. It should be voluntary past a certain number of reasonable hours you're requiring of your people, even if it's 50 or 60 instead of the average 40. That's still a long way from 80, and your entire work staff will appreciate it when you cut them the slack they're desperately trying to tell you they need even if they aren't saying it out loud. Their families will thank you, too.

LESSON 79 ★ Involve Families with the Business

Hearts and minds need to stay strong, and that makes me a big believer in getting the home family involved with the work family as much as possible. The business owner should hold four events a year, one every quarter, where your employees bring their spouses or significant others and their kids or friends into the company for fun family events—company picnics/ BBQs, go-karting, bowling, etc. That stuff is just plain fun and you also to get to know your co-workers outside of the office and you'll enjoy watching their families interact. That spirit then becomes woven into your corporate culture. Your employees will be happier workers and their significant others more understanding when they have to stay late and put in the longer hours or bring work home with them.

For most of us, our families come first. But even if you're a younger entrepreneur or junior leader who hasn't started one yet, this rule still applies to you. Spend your weekends sailing or riding bikes or racing cars or hunting or fishing, or in whatever activity you prefer. It rejuvenates you and protects you from working yourself so hard that the product of your efforts becomes inferior because you've been pushing yourself too hard. You can do higher quality work when you give yourselves the break you need.

LESSON 81 ★ Eat with Your Family

Consider a cover story published recently by *The Atlantic* which acknowledged the reality that "sadly, Americans rarely eat together anymore. In fact, the average American eats one in every five meals in her car, one in four Americans eats at least one fast food meal every single day, and the majority of American families report eating a single meal together less than five days a week. It's a pity that so many Americans are missing out on what could be meaningful time with their loved ones, but it's even more than that. Not eating together also has quantifiably negative effects both physically and psychologically."[73]

When your children are young, spend quality time with them at home. Putting down my smart phone to spend an hour a night playing video games (we played Mario Kart™), shooting BB guns, walking our dog, or playing guitar and drums with the kids let them know how much I loved them. The time I spent with them and my beautiful wife was priceless and added value to my work life at the same time. Once I was back at the office, I didn't want to lose sight of my #1 priority: my family.

Of course, as professionals, we work to support our families, which gives us meaning, but to achieve a healthy work/life balance you have to spend time and not just money on the people you're working for.

It sounds obvious, but don't take my word for it; take *Fortune* magazine's word, which recently reported, "working fathers who see their children daily are more satisfied with their jobs and less likely to resign, according to a new study. The findings, to be published in the *Academy of Management Perspectives,* suggests that companies should allow working fathers time with family as way to increase employee retention."[74]

LESSON 82 ★ Lead by Example

So you can't screw up that work/family priority, ever, and if the core values at your company are aligned with your personal values, as they should be, then your culture should encourage you and your employees to spend quality time with your families. Your children take their cues from you regarding what quality time really means; at work, it's much the same: your employees are taking their cues from you on how much time they can promise their families at home.

[73] https://www.theatlantic.com/health/archive/2014/07/the-importance-of-eating-together/374256
[74] http://fortune.com/2015/01/09/fathers-children-work

If you're a business owner or leader who leads by example, they'll gladly follow you out the door at night. And I guarantee you'll all show up the next morning recharged and ready to work that much harder for the company.

According to *Forbes*, this is known as **The Ripple Effect,** wherein "there is a knock-on or ripple effect when employees take time away from the office. Employees come back to work after time away more refreshed and productive. In addition, time away from work reduces stress. Employees with reduced stress tend to be healthier. Healthier employees tend to be more engaged. Engaged employees create happy enthused customers.
Happier customers come back more often and bring their friends. Repeat customers and referrals create a strong bottom line."[75]

By encouraging a strong work-life balance as part of your core values, your business will thrive because your employees are thriving, creating a well-rounded life for everyone.

Going through the trials and tribulations of being a business owner or leader is going to be stressful not only for you but for your staff as well—especially when you're first starting out or landing a new client that requires putting in extra hours, whether at the office or once you get home. You're simply going to have to sacrifice. The thing you want to make sure you don't sacrifice on a regular basis is that precious time with your family. Better to spend time with them, then go back to work (if you absolutely must…) after they go to bed at 9, or if you can work from home, do that. That's much better than the quick pop-in.

Spending two hours a night with your family in the evening has always been the advice I've been given and seen work in my own family, and it's the same advice I recommend to my clients too. Whether you help your kid solve the math problem or not doesn't matter; she'll still appreciate the time you spent trying to help. If you leave the office at 4 p.m. to go to your kid's Little League game or your daughter's gymnastics meet, they'll feel like they won either way because you were on the sideline rooting them on.

That said, it's important for the entrepreneur class to draw the distinction between leading a well-rounded life, which makes more sense, vs. having what is traditionally termed in Corporate America as a "work/life balance." Theoretically, if the work you do is energizing, fulfilling, provides a decent living, makes you happy and makes other people happy, then it's not likely "Oh God, now I've got to go to the office," when you walk out the door in the

[75] https://www.forbes.com/sites/stanphelps/2015/06/16/three-things-richard-branson-knows-about-time-away-from-the-office/#27056f436fd9
[76] http://www.nytimes.com/2013/02/10/opinion/sunday/relax-youll-be-more-productive.html

morning. You're more likely skipping out the door, saying, "I get to go to the office, do my thing, and be with my people." When you head home at night, you're not so tired that you have to fake it with your family because you've been seamlessly doing your thing at work.

Nevertheless, you have to keep your eyes open to make sure you're giving quality time to both. *The New York Times* pointed out, "that the *energy* employees bring to their jobs is far more important in terms of the value of their work than is the number of hours they work. By managing energy more skillfully, it's possible to get more done, in less time, more sustainably."[76]

Let me double down on the fact that, as part of the aforementioned strategy, your time away from the office MUST include at least one family vacation where you avoid all work during "family" hours, and if you absolutely have to work while you're away, get up early and get it out of the way while your family's still asleep. Better yet, let your team back at the office cover your day-to-day activities so expertly because you've trained them and trust them. Make sure to give them the right amount of their own R&R with their families, so when you're on yours you can totally unplug, knowing they have you covered.

When you're with your family, shut off your smartphone, focus on your spouse and your kids, and ask them to do the same. Make time for your family; make sure they have the same priority as your work commitments. Make a schedule of family time events that can't be easily changed or moved. Instead of planning for business success, you'll be planning for family success. I find it amazing how much we plan for business and other outside-of-the-home interests, but how little we plan, define and share a vision for who and what we want to be a as family. You'll find that It's an invaluable planning tool, especially if you have a busy family each where everyone's trying to make time for *you*. You don't have to regiment your whole life to it, but it comes in very handy in making sure that everyone in the family is making time for each other, heading in the right direction and taking their cues from you as they always will.

After a long career and decent amount of time on this earth, you don't want your headstone to read: "This Guy Holds the Record for Most TPS Reports Produced in a Day." I know I'd feel sorry for that guy if I walked past his headstone. What you want it to read is something along the lines of: "Beloved father, husband, son, and brother, friend to all, always inspiring, giving and helping others." I can tell you right now that one of my final goals in life is that I really screw up traffic in my town when I die. I want the whole city to be late for work because so many people came to pay their respects to me. And that's because I earned their respect and admiration for doing a lot of beneficial and uplifting things for scores of people. A legacy of making positive impacts on others not simply acquiring wealth is my mission in life.

The last lesson I wish to reinforce is the importance of taking care of yourself as well as you take care of your business. A healthy home life means a healthy work life—it's that simple. We often get so wrapped up in working hard that we forget who we're really doing all that work for: our families. I know I've fell victim to it myself more than a few times. So you have to make sure you budget in enough time to spend with the people you're doing all this for, so that your work/life balance is kept in a healthy state. When you do that, you'll not only come in every morning to a happy work environment; you'll also leave the office for a happy home at the end of every day. Remember, your family will be more committed to you as an entrepreneur or business leader when your work isn't zapping all your energy but rather energizing and fulfilling you. You're a much stronger business operator when you have that balance.

This approach to work/life balance is always verified by family members. I've even occasionally had employees and client's wives or husbands look me right in the eye and thank me for the positive changes that are paying dividends in their families. This is about the greatest feeling that I get in my work when I can help people with the "important stuff" in life that really makes a difference to them and their loved ones. This is not a change that can be made overnight in your business or at home. Long road marches are not done in single steps, as they say in the military, but the time invested in that journey will pay dividends that you cannot underestimate.

Lastly, I'd like to discuss some of the many outlets and resources that will help you be a better you. Over the years I've been turned on to these by peers and mentors, and I've had the opportunity to experience them all at some point. I'll tell you right now how life changing and positive they have been for me, so consider them for yourself and see which ones can help fill in the missing pieces of your ideal life.

1. A Peer Group

Here are just a few: (EO) Entrepreneurs Organization, (YPO) Young Presidents Organization, and Vistage. Most of these business owner peer-to-peer groups also have special groups or "forums" for their senior leaders to attend as well. At a peer group, it's about the entrepreneur or senior leader rather than the industry. Here you will find others facing the same day-to-day challenges and pressures that you face. With learning events, retreats, lunch and learns, and social events there are many great ways to participate. By sharing past experiences and having a safe place to unload and unpack some of your business and personal baggage, you will gain valuable perspective, understanding, and confidence.

2. A Hobby or Club

It is very important to have time to unplug from your normal routine and do something that energizes you and gives you joy. Lots of people who work with their minds all day love to work with their hands; I like to paint, play music, and keep my marksmanship skills sharp.

3. Personal Coaching

An accountability coach, a life coach, professional therapy, whatever you need that you can't seem to get or figure out for yourself many have found here.

4. A Fitness Routine

When you look and feel great you'll be more likely to do great. When you're tired, stressed, overweight, feeling self-conscious or depressed, it's much more difficult to do great. Working out has many proven positive side effects, when you make it a habit it just gets done, so make it a part of a daily routine, and after a while it becomes part of your life. I like to exercise early in the morning, so I have the energy, and the crazy day ahead won't get in the way of the workout.

5. Big Bucket List Vacations

The let's-save-up-and-dream-big kind of vacation is always something that gives me a big goal to work up to, and hitting goals and then celebrating is what is success is all about. Too many people die with lots of money in their bank accounts and not enough of these "once in a lifetime" experiences. Think about what your regrets would be if you knew today was going to be your last day. Write them down, then start forging a plan to knock a few of those off your list in the next few years!

6. Three or Four-Day Weekends

These are the best for me, as I have a limited schedule and attention span and two or three nights somewhere within a quick flight or driving distance, or some really cool day trips are also great. These getaways are much easier to schedule and are much more affordable. The concept of "staycations" are also super fun, where you stay home but put up a tent in the backyard or do touristy stuff in your community that you wouldn't normally do. Projecting movies on to an outside wall at our house and inviting friends over during nice weather is one of my favorites!

7. Service to your Community

Volunteering at a great charitable cause that resonates with you, participating in local politics, school boards, or churches are a great way to give back the community that supports your business. I give my time to several organizations that help others in need, and it makes me feel great!

8. Be a Mentor to Someone

Think about all the people who have helped you become you? Most people have had some influential mentors help them climb to wherever they are today. Send the elevator back down for the next person. I've found that when I'm teaching others, I'm re-enforcing what I need to be mindful of as well. When you have an abundance mindset and share your gifts openly with others you always get plenty in return, vs. having a scarcity mindset and not wanting to "lose" or share what you have somehow gained. In my experience, abundance-minded people are much happier and content vs. scarcity-minded people, who somehow always don't seem to have enough and generally have negative outlook in nature. Life is way too short; choose your mindset carefully!

 **8-POINT CHECKLIST**

All the things biz owners and leaders need to be their very best.

---

1. Peer group that you have selected. _____

You'll need to give it some time to integrate into the chapter, and join a forum (a small tight-knit subset of group that you'll share deeply with).

2. Hobby or Club that you have chosen. _____

Are you getting the joy and happiness you desired from this activity?

Are you able to share this with another? _____

3. Personal Coaching/Therapy option. _____

Are you seeing the investment of your time and money come to fruition?

_____

What's the biggest mindset shift you have experienced?_____

_____

What are your goals for the future? _____

_____

4. Fitness Routine that you have selected? _____

What are the days and times that you have committed to maintain a healthy mind and body? _____

(Mornings are recommended as the day can easily get away from you compromising your fitness time later in the day)

5. Big vacations ideas that inspire, reset, relax, and energize you. _____

_____

What is your timeline to travel? _____

Have you planed how you will pay for this vacation? _____

Are you travelling with your significant other, or are you bringing other family and friends? _____

6. Mini Vacations/Staycations. Four or more per year are recommended. What ideas do you have? _____

_____

Do you have them scheduled, so you don't book work activities and blow the concept of unplugging and refreshing? _____

7. Service to your community. Have you selected a charity that fits with you and your family's interests and passions? _____

How does this make you feel? _____

Can you scale this passion to help others? _____

8 Mentor another person. If you could mentor a junior "You," what did you have the hardest time with on your way up? _____

_____

How could you provide insight, encouragement, and support to help another accelerate their trajectory? _____

_____

What I've learned over the years is when you have covered these bases, it's really hard not to feel like a million dollars, because you are giving so much to you and those close to you. I was a Taker for many years, once I became a Giver, life simply smelled a little sweeter for me.

Take a deep breath!

ARE YOU READY TO ENLIST?

Now, are you ready to enlist in this new mindset? It may be one of the most personal questions you'll ever ask yourself, because you haven't finished reading an impersonal field manual with a bunch of standardized instructions for you to carry out. Rather, this book has been a call-to-arms, a code to follow, a mission that can only be successfully pursued through conviction, discipline, and vision. If you have the courage to see it through, if you follow the steps in this field manual to the T, you will achieve greater and greater victories on the business battlefield and ultimately life itself.

But first, let me come to attention and salute you for finishing this field manual! The reason you opened this book in the first place, let alone read it all the way through, is because you're trying to be a better leader for everyone in your organization. A strong and capable leader is what your troops want you to be, and that's who you need to be every day you walk in the office door.

I know. Easier said than done, right? That's why I'm the Business Sergeant— to help you fuse my military leadership training into business leadership. If you're just starting this process right now, you should consider yourself a Business Private, but if you dedicate yourself to my approach, before you know it you'll be wearing my stripes on your arm. You'll develop the confidence to execute to the highest standard, to build a team so loyal that they'll gladly do whatever it takes to get there. You're going to modify your current approach into a more active, intentional, fired-up, inspirational leadership style so you can execute on the business battlefield with military level precision, and have lots of fun along the way!

That is something that I haven't covered yet, but I'll hit it right now. When I served in uniform, it wasn't all business. We had an exciting and fun time together, we had a bond that was forged in both the good times and the tough times. The fellowship, camaraderie, and unit pride are things that many veterans after leaving uniform really, really miss and that's because that feeling isn't easily found or created. That, in essence, is what I'm talking about in this field manual, for you to create such a place that will be spoken of with great pride and admiration for years to come. The opposite of ordinary is extraordinary, and in order to create such an environment, you'll need to be having epic levels of fun. The fun happens naturally when you have assembled the right team and given them the right tools to be successful. Your job as the leader is to make sure you keep things light enough to keep the fun in everything that you do, while still getting the mission accomplished.

I've practiced the strategic alliance of military and business principles for many years now, with plenty of stumbles, fumbles, and learning curves along the way, and the key to my success has been in motivating and managing the best out of the troops on my teams. You can do the same only when you discover what your "why" is and what motivates you as the leader of your unit. I came from humble beginnings and didn't like growing up that way. Nor did I want the same for my family, so my bottom line philosophy has always remained the same: if you don't like something, then step up and change it! Don't whine, don't complain, but pull yourself up by the bootstraps, put your nose to the grindstone, (insert whatever cliché you want here), but just do it! That's been my mentality the whole way, and I appreciate hardships of the past because they gave me this perspective. Those hard times were immensely valuable to me, although at the time I didn't think they had any value.

Our struggles are what forge our fortitude and perseverance in life, and if you have a go-to mindset, you will eventually get to your destination. On paper, I shouldn't be anywhere near as successful as I've managed to become in life. I happen to believe that scrappy, resourceful, and resilient people in business like myself, who don't have an MBA from Harvard, can still walk into a room and command the attention and respect. I was fortunate to have a lot of mentors along the way, and I wasn't afraid to take risks and fail. While failure shouldn't be a badge of honor on anyone's arm, we must remember that failure provides you with an invaluable perspective. Many of the business owners I work with have had years of nothing but success. They don't know the other side, or even how close they've come to failure. My job as the Business Sergeant is to open their eyes to that risk and help them avoid it, while helping them become a stronger, more efficient, and profitable operation in the long run.

With all that said, every successful military training exercise has a review at its conclusion, so I now want to take the opportunity to touch on everything we've covered in this Field Manual.

Number One is reinforcing the importance of commitment. You've heard me go on about this time and again throughout our sojourn together, but I still can't say it enough. You can't be half-pregnant, as the timelessly sage saying goes, so you have to remember to always hold your team 100% accountable to the commitment that they have made to you and the rest of the team, even when that makes them somewhat uncomfortable. Which leads me to propose a final mirror moment where you can ask yourself: "Am I truly 100% committed to my troops' well-being and development, to the great responsibility of leading other people that comes with the top spot?"

There's another classic axiom that's been flying around the military for years, having originated among pilots: "There's two types of pilots you'll meet: BOLD pilots, and OLD pilots, but you'll never meet an Old, Bold Pilot." Point is, you'll have to be very careful when doing bold stuff in business, so you can survive and become an old pilot with some cool stories to tell. As captain of your crew, which one do you want to be? Even though the saying implies that you can't be both, I think you just need to be aware when things get tricky, and know your limits and those of the people that you have surrounded yourself with. The difference between crashing that plane and staying in flight for many profitable years is ultimately up to you. If you're a brave pilot making bold business maneuvers, put some safety guidelines in place, that way you will confidently inspire the rest of your squad to be proud wingmen and wingwomen who will follow you anywhere on the ground and in the air.

This brings into focus another central tenet that weaves its way through every chapter in this field manual—the LACK of great leadership currently driving today's corporate culture and workforce. There aren't a lot of examples of great leadership for people to follow and model. I firmly believe that the typical H.R. department has wussified and neutered great leaders to the point where they disengage themselves. Time and again, I've found people sitting in leadership seats who at heart want nothing to do with the responsibility that great leadership demands. By all means follow employment law, protect your people, and do the right thing even when no one is looking, but ask yourself often, "is this acceptable? Do I have to tolerate this behavior? What are my options?"

When you're afraid to take the lead as a business owner, it can cripple you faster than a lack of commitment. The two are inextricably tied to the success of any company, from the top down or bottom up. So, if you're not 100% of the leader you can and need to be, it's time to step up and become one NOW.

As your vision comes together and you find non-believers on your team, you now have the strength to liberate them and allow them to find their correct unit. By replacing them with people who want to be in your unit, you'll quickly have a more committed team and thus more committed customers. Once you have the right people in the right seats, people who are accountable to each other and getting more done than ever before—in part because they see how you're no longer willing to put up with any bullshit in the office—your team will be executing like a well-oiled military unit. Your strategic partnerships are sound, you're gaining more new ground with and for your clients than ever before, and everyone is happier with healthy relationships and results all around.

And now that you know what kind of troops you want on your team, ask yourself, "AM I READY TO BE A BUSINESS SERGEANT?"

It will take time to fully grow into that version of yourself. But even if you only take a few ideas of what we've discussed here and apply it, you'll still be much stronger as a company than before. The bottom line is that the ideas and methods in this book will work for you. I've seen it happen too many times over many years to have any doubt about that!

I would love to hear from readers who have successfully implemented some or all of the systems and steps in this book. The greatest reward for me is to see people take control of their own destiny and make their vision a reality. Always remember, at the end of the day YOU'RE IN CONTROL, so if you don't like the way something looks in your culture, CHANGE IT!

Stop talking about it and make it happen, because all you have to do to enlist in this army is believe in yourself, your team, and **become the BUSINESS SERGEANT you were born to be!**

For more information and content, please visit www.bizsgt.com

NOTES

ACTION ITEMS